THE LAST GOOD

WATER

GREAT LAKES BOOKS

A complete listing of the books in this series can be found at the back of this volume.

Philip P. Mason, Editor
Department of History, Wayne State University

Dr. Charles K. Hyde, Associate Editor
Department of History, Wayne State University

THE LAST GOOD

WATER

prose and poetry, 1988–2003

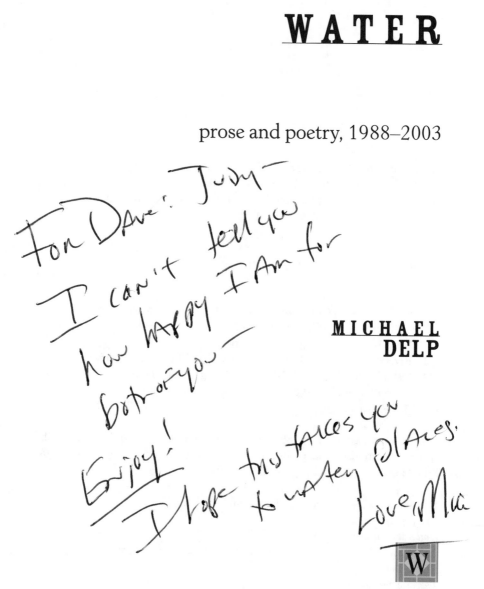

MICHAEL DELP

For Dave: Judy —
I can't tell you
how happy I am for
both of you —
Enjoy!
I hope this takes you
to watery places.
Love, Mia

Wayne State University Press   Detroit

Library of Congress Cataloging-in-Publication Data

Delp, Michael.
    The last good water : prose and poetry, 1988–2003 / Michael Delp.
       p.   cm.   —   (Great Lakes books)
    ISBN 0-8143-3171-8 (pbk. : alk. paper)
  1. Rivers—Poetry.   2. Fishing—Poetry.   3. Michigan—Poetry.
  4. Fishing—Michigan.   5. Rivers—Michigan.   I. Title.   II. Series.
    PS3554.E44447L37 2003
    811'.54—dc21   2003010724

∞ The paper used in this publication meets the minimum requirements of the
American National Standard for Information Sciences—Permanence of Paper for
Printed Library Materials, ANSI Z39.48–1984.

Some of this work has been previously published in:
Over the Graves of Horses
Under the Influence of Water
The Coast of Nowhere: Meditations on Rivers, Lakes and Streams
Riverwatch
Traverse Magazine
GLRC/NPR Commentaries

This is the way forests were in the olden days. This is about the last good country there is left. Nobody gets in here ever.

They were coming down a long hill when the saw sunlight ahead through the tree trunks. Now, at the edge of the timber there was wintergreen growing and some partridge berries and the forest floor began to be alive with growing things. Through the tree trunks they saw an open meadow that sloped to where white birches grew along the stream. Below the meadow and the line of the birches there was the dark green of a cedar swamp and far beyond the swamp there were dark blue hills. There was an arm of the lake between the swamp and the hills. But from here they could not see it. They only felt from the distances that it was there.

Ernest Hemingway, "The Last Good Country"

CONTENTS

DRIFTING THE COASTLINES

WADING THE DARKER CURRENT

WHAT IT IS

a fly-fishing manifesto

What it is, is this: after decades of fishing you come to realize that you live in a house made entirely of desire. Everything is fishing, a life given over to the obsession to be on the water, a way water has of leaking into every pore, every synapse, every fissure of bone, your marrow gone liquid. At night you hear the fly line singing, and that's exactly what it is, singing, in the living room, the line moving rhythmically past the chairs, curving around the television as if it were a river boulder.

The stairs are water, falling water, the runs and pools threaded into the risers, the places where your feet have taken you to dreams for all these years. There is water running in the house, rivers coursing in the copper lines.

In the morning, a glass of water surges from the tap and you drink the very bodies of fish into your own body. You stand in the first light glinting off the river, light which moves in streams through the windows, and your entire body shifts to fit that light, the light moving past you like water. Then the transformation, the movement of light through your eyes and into your veins and you want to gather up your rods and reels, the vest and flies, leave the house and dissolve away.

What it is, is your body becoming like the rivers you fish. You dream that your heart has its own desires: that it can call you in, and that when you enter the heart chambers, the map of every river you've ever fished rolls out under your feet, the landscape falling like rain into place; the desire to fish always on your lips, each word marked by the sound of moving water, the river in each fleck of your eyes.

What it is, is to know that the rivers are haunted. That someday your father will be on the river exactly where he said he'd meet you. Your grandfather will be there too, and the dead friends who gave you their desire to fish like a man hands over a chalice to the man he leaves behind. All their graves will be empty.

What it is, is to know a way inside. That your mind travels down the line, through the fly, past the hook into the water and back through your feet, entering your head cleaner, wider, the river a thread, a rope, a knotless strand of silk.

Back at the house it is still desire in the rooms, desire rising in your wife, and daughter, the way their eyes flash, the retinas moist, wet, a thin film of water between you and what they see in you. What it is, is to lift them up and take them outside, tell them to lean close to your chest and listen: a heart running to catch up with the cataracts it creates.

What it is, is to know that you die going in, you die going under and you die on the bottom. But your body stays there, then sifts away. They won't find you. They will search for days, find your rod, your hat maybe, even a piece of the sandwich you didn't finish, a half-empty shot of whiskey in the deep bend you named after your daughter. They will grieve and wait there on the shore for days, weeks, standing in all kinds of weather and they will leave flowers for you, trinkets, messages written on birch bark. They will call up and down the river and some of them may see your ghost in the cedars. They will think you have gone for good, that you have taken up residence in a place marked by wild rivers, wild fish, a place only dreamed of. But what it is, finally, is to know that your heart is water itself. Always has been. But they will come to that slowly, when they wake at night in the house and hear the ghost line humming over their heads and feel something wild and pulsing, surging in their own hearts.

THE MANIFESTO
OF RIVERS

BUILDING RIVERS

First, you will need all the desire you can conjure up from your bone marrow, every ounce of blood that feels as if you woke in the night and found yourself made of rain, the clear water-blood of storms. You will need a mind purified by the slow percolation of the very idea of water, each notion of rivers sifting through your mind like a bubble through honey. What you have understood as love all your life will now be given over to the steady rhythm of the seasons: the sharp smell of October as you cup your hands to drink, then, the shift and heave of ice and snow, the slow patience of spring moving north; the miracle of summer singing into your skin. Begin with secret water: the bubbling water of swamps and hummocks, as if it came forth speaking itself into existence, and you were there to make the way.

As for your body, you will require the iron back of a god, muscles churning like waves under your skin, supple enough for the task, the days of lifting, digging, cutting close to bedrock, always then the urge to bend again and again to the work, the fluid thought of the river that is coming, flowing out of your head, a river dream pulsing out of your fingers.

You will need the inner sense to follow contours, know the way the glacier caressed the moraines and kettles into being, turned pastures into valleys, how it left drinks of water for the dry ground. You will have to possess a cartographer's patience to find the height of land and then the long, gradual gradient, knowing that the river always leaves itself behind, then runs to catch up with where it has to go. You will need things from the earth: rocks, pebbles, stones, boulders, specific kinds of silt and loam, clay strong enough to withstand the fists of water. You must possess the wisdom to know that where you place anything will not be where it will stay, the river pushing tangled clots of ice and debris down its long, narrow bed.

And you will need plants, huge trees, oaks and pines, the soft arms of willows, wild iris, lilacs and honeysuckle. Tag alders, and every kind of fern, sweet bracken, their green stalks mingling with a thousand kinds of grasses. And you will also need sky. An immense ribbon of sky to lift up like a blue tent over the entire length of the river, most of it barely visible in the web of tree branches and deadfall on each bank, like a promise hovering in the air. A place for the moon and sun to hang, one to bake the river, the other to cool the nights, bring the insects out, millions and millions of them, enough species for a library of books. Hatches, emergences and spinner falls, the dark clouds of their wings, falling spent out of the sky like rain. You will need watercress and choke cherry, a nation of algae and a million cedar trees, bent and twisted at the edge of every pool.

You will need the ability to walk and keep walking, honing your work, the sense of flow pushing at you as if your mind were some kind of compass, the needle an arrow pointing the way.

And then, you will need fish, browns the size of footballs, their eyes dark from hiding, brook trout to fit perfectly in your hand, their colors borrowed from parts of the sky, the iridescent rocks of planets, and rainbows spawned at the Godhead of colors.

But mostly you will need hearts, hearts alchemized from the soul of some crazed sorcerer: an epiphany of hearts. Wild hearts in wild fish, their chambers clean as sluices, their blood mingled with bits of stars, and wild dust dredged up from the last reaches of time.

And when you are through, when you have cut and dragged and turned every deep bend, you will have purified your own heart, a sluice itself, sending your own wild blood out into your eyes that look across the surface of the river, your body part of the places you have made, reading the book of the water, each stone a word polished by the tongue of the river.

INNER FISHING

Better than anything I know, trout fishing serves as a pause, a deep breath in the crush of living. It is a deceptive form of enlightenment: it seems incredibly simple, yet trout fishing illuminates an inner life, asks the mind and body to give themselves over to another power. It requires, as do most forms of enlightenment, a long period of careful study, pain and suffering, passion, a manic devotion to ritual, and the mastery of a series of subtle moves.

The long study for most trout fishermen means an entire childhood with only glimpses of trout streams. Instead, you are spirited off to bluegill ponds and given the traditional cane pole and bobber or an incredibly inexpensive Zebco rod and reel. You spend your first ten years digging for worms, trudging through tall grass in search of warm water ponds, and rowing the boat for your father. The trout stream is only a fantasy concocted out of the smells and images drifting out of your father's old fishing vest.

Initiation into the world of trout fishing comes subtly. At first, the old man is careful to let you only "touch" the bamboo rod. Later, he will let you land a fish or two, but always with his hands firmly wrapped around yours.

The novice enters the world of trouting as a heathen. Your hands are bloodied by the deaths of countless nightcrawlers and by the sure knowledge of how to hook a frog through the lips to catch bass. Salvation finally arrives at your twelfth or thirteenth Christmas. Your first flyrod, usually fiberglass and indestructible, weighs heavy in your hands. The reel is a single-action cheapy that looks good but is hardly a match for your father's lightweight heirloom. You borrow his rusty flies, or scoop them out of the wastebasket after they have been chewed to uselessness by huge fish.

Your movements on the stream are awkward, a ragged imitation of the master angler in your mind. You begin the long process of learning to read streams. Secrets are revealed in current patterns and in the way water piles up around rocks. There are early mornings filled with fog and mist, summers spent smelling cedar swamps and rain-swollen streams. You begin thinking, dreaming, talking constantly of trout.

Now begins the minute cataloging of stream details. You find a favorite stretch of water and fish it for weeks on end, carrying home new details to add to the imaginary stream you are building in your mind.

Later, this dream-born trout stream will be complete, a place to retreat into and fish over and over. For now, you dissect, analyze, and at nineteen or twenty call yourself an angler.

After countless pairs of leaky waders you know well the cost in terms of human comfort: inhaling thousands of insects, learning to smoke lousy cigars to keep them away, and absorbing gallons of ice-cold rainwater. Too often you will spend twenty dollars on the wrong flies or find yourself stumbling along a river in the dark with a fly stuck in your forehead.

Yet the imaginary stream grows more detailed. Without realizing it, when you are depressed, your mind takes you there. The water has become an old, familiar place and you watch yourself practice the correct presentation of the fly, putting all twenty-five or thirty years of your experience into the cast of the line.

In your quest for fishing mastery you will admit to being a manic fisherman. You wake in the middle of the night and check the calendar for the trout opener, check and recheck your gear, and spend more time with your wife so you can bargain for a few more minutes of being late in the summer. All your fishing movement is the observation of a perfectly contrived dance, a ritual each time you gather up your equipment and place it carefully in the car. This ritual takes on many forms. Perhaps a sip of whiskey before each outing, or tying leaders with two knots always in the same place. Perhaps it's the way you take the rod out of its case and push it together, gently, aiming the guides as though targeting an imaginary fish. The entire sequence becomes second nature, something to hand down to a son or daughter, something to give your life a kind of permanence and clarity.

At forty-five or fifty you feel you have mastered the sport. All the ritual and suffering, the intense passion of hooking and netting fish, accumulates on your inner stream. Each movement of the rod becomes a movement of your entire body. On those bright autumn days there is no difference between you and the stream. Even at home, when you add a small detail to the interior stretch of water, you feel the way your legs go numb in your waders. You have passed from a boy who merely wished for a fly to land somewhere near a fish to a bundle of sinew and nerves aimed not only at fishing, but also at the purity trout fishing offers.

So it is that years later, when you finally give your equipment to a young disciple, you will still be able to feel the tug of line in your arm. It all adds up, the study, pain, intense pleasure, practicing the ritual. We get where we are not by where we want to go or by where we've been, but by what we do with each moment. On the inner stream time ceases, for memory makes no distinction as to the coming and passing of seasons. The stream is always open, the slicks and runs exactly where you first started to construct them as a boy.

You stand on the edge of this mental flowing of water, slide in and take that first, quick breath in the cold water. Once again you feel that old electricity. You end the pilgrimage where it began. You complete the circle, are part of the circle, and when you move, the inner stream moves with you.

RIVERDOG

What you need is to get over here on the river and live like a dog.

Dave Lemmen

In July of 1949, six months after my baptism, my grandfather carried me into the water of Bass Lake. As my mother tells it, he knelt there in the darkness and filtered palms of lake water over my legs, motioning with his hands toward islands, drop-offs and his best fishing spots. For years I drifted the lake with him and my father, casting our plugs toward shore, the Bible music from Camp Concordia countering our low whispers for the fish gods to send us luck. Later, in my teens, after the cottage sold, I cruised town with my buddies, the notions of water seemingly unimportant when compared to the bodies of cheerleaders and the grail of beer.

Twenty-one years later and newly married, I headed north to teach and live in northern Michigan. Looking back, I know that juncture, that place where my life, which could have gone anywhere, took a defining turn toward a life on the water. I grew up a lake boy, but was always looking toward brushy creeks and farm streams hoping to see a glimpse of a brook trout, not content with catching bass and panfish. I wanted trout, wanted to enter that vaulted world of fly-fishing, wicker creels and bamboo rods. What I sense now, in my mid-forties, is that what I really wanted was always to be in the presence of rivers. I wanted to become a riverdog, smelling of cedar swamps, river mud, my face lined from month after month of living on the water.

I am convinced now, after spending a good many days on trout streams, that rivers come from the veins of the gods themselves. Surely, rivers are the blood of the beings more capable and sensible than we are and to stand waist deep in a trout stream is to make contact with the pure spirit of the gods themselves. Not true of lakes, literal bowls of water lodged in the earth.

Through turns of fate, I have lived on lakes for years and find them fairly uninteresting in their containment when compared to the coursing motion of the moving water of rivers. If a man can "seldom be appeased by house current after he has been hit by lightning," then my life spent on lakes is the equivalent of sucking on a couple of "D" cells. True, I have watched lakes for hours, heaving and churning in storms, but there is always the idea that the water never leaves. Put your soul afloat on a lake and you'll likely get it back. Do the same on a river and you'll be able to let yourself drift away for good.

The movement of rivers is fundamental to their power for me. Learning a river is a textual process. Go to a river as you would a text and you'll likely learn far more than attending a lifetime of cocktail parties, sales meetings, task force initiatives or MFA courses. On a given trout stream there are thousands of bits of information constantly changing and rearranging themselves; the movements of fish hidden under the surface, the face of the river always offering up a mirror of the sky.

Even more powerful for me is the notion that being in a river has something to do with the process of letting the crush of the world sift out of you. Countless times I have let go of cars that won't start, mountains of debt, the bitter taste of arguments. Each time the river takes the debris of my life away. And when I turn to look upstream, there is almost always something floating down to me that I thought I had lost forever. I have seen the ghosts of ancestors along the river and I have seen myself standing under the shade of sweeping cedars, always the words of admonition coming from my ghost mouth to cash it in and give myself over to water.

Lately, I've been fantasizing about doing just that. I'm haunted by an old photograph from the late 1800s of a salmon king on the Columbia River. Once a year, the chief would don a ceremonial suit made entirely of salmon skins, his arms stretching over the water calling to the sky for a bountiful harvest of fish.

In my waking dreams I see myself standing in the doorway of a ramshackle cabin, the deep light of an October afternoon glinting off the scales of my brook trout skin shirt. I'd long since have changed my name to Muddler or Matuka and would have risen each day to a breakfast of fresh brook trout. My eyes would see clearly once more, surely I could see in all directions, the trout in me looking up at the moon, a milky disk, even farther from the world of men.

CASTING: A MEDITATION

Something pushes me out the door and into foul weather. If pressed to identify the force, I might realize it comes from the throbbing in my temples, the beast of sitting in too many meetings. Or it might be the grip a nightmare life has on my imagination that makes me head for the river.

It is almost dark. Cold. Bits of rain and snow are falling. After five minutes in the water my hands stiffen, the wind rising to a low moan. I begin the ritual I've followed for over twenty years. No mantra here, only the rhythmic swish of my line cutting through the weather. I've casted this way for hours, years if you added them all up, and now, I find myself casting nowhere in particular to no fish in particular. Just casting. For all I know, with this collection of bad dreams festering in my head, I could be fishing for old tires. No matter. When it gets completely dark, I'm still at it, the line invisible now as it lifts and sings through the air.

I begin thinking to myself about the nature of the line, asking what it's really doing out there in the dark. If it were finer, longer, I might be able to loft it straight up into the sky, sew the constellations together. Make that direct link between Sagittarius and the North Star I've felt since birth.

Though fully awake after casting for hours, numbed by cold and repetition, I lapse into ever-specific waking dreams: out in front of me there surely is a raft of beautiful women, or maybe a bag of money floating downstream. Or I'll feel a heavy strike and miraculously recover some lost part of myself.

Finally, it comes to me that I'm really casting into the nothing of this northern Michigan night to get rid of something. Each curl of my wrist and I cast out a personal demon. Each cast and the bills and debts fall away, the car that won't start begins to vanish. But what I sense is that I can let the demons sulk there at the end of my line for only so long, then I must bring them back.

So I cast and retrieve, cast and retrieve, long into the night, praying for the line to come from deep inside me, from some pit in my belly where emptiness lives. I think of the millions of empty casts I've made, and here in the darkness they suddenly start coming back, crisscrossing over me like a net, the sky luminous, clouds meshing over the moon, each cast a vein into memory.

Later, I try to fall asleep in the cabin, my casting arm throbbing under my pillow, and all the memories of my life on the water start sifting back into my hands. I think of the very heart of casting: not how I cast, but why. I think of the metaphorical beauty of empty casts, the dark edge of faith honed by the resignation of coming up empty almost every time. And I think of how the act of casting has linked me to the men I honor. I remember my grandfather calling back over his shoulder from the front of the boat just before a lightning storm on Turk Lake. "Keep casting," he whispers. "Cast for all your worth." "Cast your heart out," he said, and I remember how he once told me that every time he made a cast he felt part of himself go free. So I cast there with him in the dream, our rhythm perfect. He stands in the bow, casting under the lightning, the bass cruising like phantoms under the boat, his rod etched with light.

RIVER GODS

You may have heard this story. Maybe a long time ago. Maybe it was in a little café with a few old calendars askew on the walls, some gut-busting eggs frying on the back griddle. But when you heard it, you knew it was legend.

It was a story about going to the river every spring. He was almost sixty the last time he did it, he said. He had fished the same water for five decades with his grandfather and his father. They called it "their" water. The rituals were carried out meticulously each season: opening-day breakfast, checking the gear, exchanging small presents, then the walk to the river. And after both of them had died, he kept a secret, he said, something he always did in private, always at the same spot where the creek fed into the mainstream.

He had borrowed this, he was saying. Borrowed this part of his own private ritual from an Aborigine tribe in Australia. It was something about respect, about giving yourself over. He always used the same knife, he said, and pulled an old Boy Scout jackknife out of his front pocket.

Then he showed the motion he used. Not a quick slice over his wrist but a slow, delicate draw over his forearm. Then he pulled up his sleeve, and the scars laced his arm. Each one small, distinct, his left forearm covered with inch-long memories.

The bleeding never lasted long, he said. Just long enough to let a little blood fall into the river. He'd mix it slowly with his hand, then wave it along. He never said anything, only watched the way the blood swirled into the clear water, then dissolved, disappeared, became river. Twenty seasons. Twenty cuts.

After he left, I looked at my own smooth forearm, thought of the rivers I knew, the dream rivers I fished in my sleep, rivers full of mermaids, phantoms. And that day, after I heard his story, I found an old Barlow knife my father had given me at Hartwick Pines and cleaned it up.

It was there in the basement, halfway into early morning, that I felt the edge, honed perfectly. And I thought about the small gods who bless rivers, the ones who bless our fishing lives, the ones who bless our hands, the ones who bless each drop of water. I thought of my life somehow transported into each one of their favors. I thought of heading out in April, through early mist, perhaps the apparitions of ghost relatives, or the visions of waking dreams, lining the path to the river. I knew the exact spot near the AuSable over a pure spring where I would kneel down, roll up my sleeve, and make the cut, begin the process of giving myself over.

TROLLING FOR HOME

THE LANGUAGE OF WATER

1

My father knew the movements of water,
the way it held fast,
then curled around rocks in the river.
He could judge the depth of a lake
by the faint edge of darkness
he saw in the water
looking down over the side of the boat.
Today, I went fishing alone,
and held my head out over the water.
I looked at my face, his face,
for a long time,
squinted beyond reflection,
then swirled the lake with my hand,
waiting for the surface to grow darker,
give way, then go calm,
this face growing back slowly.

2

Sometimes at night
I go out on the grass,
put my ear to the ground and listen.
Three days ago
this water fell out of the sky,
a week from now it will rise back
into the air.
Branch water, well water,
creek water, root water,
the water of thunderstorms.
I press closer, listen.
Somewhere, water is falling,
rising,
and in the dream I will have of falling and rising,
I will wake again and again,
a man baptized constantly
by the voices of water.

FISHING FOR THE DEAD

For an hour I sit in the shanty
staring down into
a small hole in the ice,
my back and arms strained
from holding the spear.
In this small darkness
I feel the heat from
the kerosene stove
ricochet off the walls,
then listen for the thrust
of lake ice pushing
against itself.
I look down into
a kind of clear green sky,
a few fish drifting by like clouds.
The ice pushing against ice begins to
sound like some kind of song,
old voices
echoing back and forth across the lake,
and when I put my spear down,
move closer to the hole,
I bend my arm into a hook,
reach down through the ice,
waving it back and forth underwater,
hoping for someone to rise up,
grandfathers or uncles
washed up from the dead,
locking hands with me in some kind
of arm wrestling, knowing that to win
would mean I might bring them up
into the half-light,
whisper their names
back into their ears,
and to lose would mean

sliding my whole body through,
drifting toward bottom,
the hole in the ice above me
closing shut like an eye.

FISHING THE DREAM

1

Half-asleep
my hand begins to itch
where, hours ago,
I washed the blood from a brook trout
into the river,
and going into the dream,
I feel my hand arc,
tear away,
then circle back,
just above my line of sight,
waiting,
the great fins moving,
the eyes turned slate grey.
This was the beginning of waiting,
imagining the violence of the strike,
the bed moving,
then, limping downstairs,
the house gone icy,
thousands of fishhooks
tangled in the walls.

2

It comes over and over:
I throw my line out
through the half-mist
hanging like a second skin
over the water,
but it doesn't stop,
just keeps going,
off into the air.
Moments pass,
then minutes.
Nothing.

I poke my rod toward the wall of fog,
hoping for something out there
to take hold,
but it passes through, into nothing.
For an hour I fish the dream,
never sure where my body stops
and the molecules of fog begin.
I sit down on the bank,
try to carve enough space
for my body,
then fold myself into my knees,
knowing that the line is still out there,
the hook dragging the stillness.

3

In 1948, the year I was born,
my father rescued Stan Ash
from the Two-Hearted River
by throwing a monofilament line over him,
waited for his hand to catch,
the line to burrow in
and disappear under the flesh.
Last night I felt that line
cutting into my dream hand,
and when my father pulled me to the surface
the river suddenly widened,
and he seemed miles away.

I sat up straight in bed,
ran my finger down through the groove
of my lifeline,
felt the tug of the dream again,
one hand circling in the air,
my father on the bank,
trying to bring me in
so he could cut me free.

NIGHTFISHING AT THE HOMESTEAD DAM

We fish below the dam, the fog drifting over us,
knee-deep in water churned to white foam
while upstream a dozen fishermen line the shore
throwing their lines into what little light
falls down from a vapor lamp on the hill,
the beams from their headlamps
slicing the air as if they were coal miners
deep underground searching for drowned friends,
their voices lost in the surge of current.

In my pocket I feel for the box of lead weights
my father found in my grandfather's tackle box.
Before I tie one on I roll it in my fingers,
thinking of how his hand gripped the line,
how he told me once just before he made a cast
he wanted a small part of his life to
drift out with the line and never surface.

Tonight I am almost forty
and the sky seems to have darkened,
the stars smaller,
and each time the headlamps
drift over my face I think they have come for me,
not content with just a part of my life drifting off,
while thirty feet out I feel my line hit bottom,
the lead weight dancing like a ghost over the
        stones.

TROLLING FOR HOME

for Claudia and Jaime

I let the line slip from the reel,
fifty feet, then a hundred,
stop only for a moment,
think of setting the drag on full,
how my lure drifts just off bottom,
past the mouths of fish,
and while I row
I watch the swirls of the oars
disappear behind me.

Far away,
on the western shore,
I wait for the house light to come on.
The oars are loose in their locks,
creaking with each pull
and I begin to think of this small boat
as my body,
hollowed out, floating here
suspended above the bottom of the lake,
and so I let the line go,
imagine that I could take a filament of skin
and splice myself into the line,
let myself go out
over the back of the boat,
trailing off.

Darkness, and I forget about this life,
forget the silent breakdown of bone,
forget that I have tied my life almost invisibly
to my wife and daughter,
and that this drifting will come to something,
someplace familiar,
someplace where my body
might settle into the groove in the sand
she and her mother have made with their hands.

THE MAD ANGLER'S MANIFESTO

I speak with the voice of water,
rivulet, brook, stream and creek,
for the whitewater in lost gorges,
boiling cataracts, every place
where the souls of wild fish gather
to remind us of the power of hydrology.
I speak with the name of rain,
with the soft lips of condensation,
even the dew which gathers each night,
every drop another transition from sky to earth.
I invoke the masses of insects to take over the world,
to begin the hatching and mating sure in the fact
that tomorrow another dam will fail, another levee crumble,
another river where you live will tire of its banks
and seek retribution on your lawn,
running up your driveway and into your basement.

I praise the flash flood,
the artesian well, the flowing
hearts under our feet,
the webs of underground rivers
coursing through solid rock.

I fish in incantations, genuflections,
my body a living marker for the crest gauge,
tidal fluctuation, flood tides and fresh water seiches.
When my eye falls on rivers I praise their transparency,
their nature of shaping their way as they move.

Water is my heart churning in a white hydraulic,
my tongue longing for a quiet pool, the skin of night
settling in, mayflies on the edge of moonlight
sifting out of the trees.
I praise the lust for emergences,
the urge to quit the job, convert the pension funds to
river frontage, the sudden impulse to carry the flyrod

into a meeting, the fly ripping the lips of your superiors.
I embrace the chant of waterfalls, the litany of holy rivers:
Battenkill, Firehole, Bighorn.

I trust only the sweet smell of rotting cedar,
the scent of mudbanks festering with nymphs,
the rivers rising in my blood like an illness, a fever sent by
the god of desire to make his presence known, something jolting
through the veins to replace the done deal, the raise with a
corner office, the soul trader you most likely have become.

THE DREAM OF THE MAD ANGLER

My flesh was water,
and when I stepped into the river
I disappeared.
I drank moonlight in the dark
and whispered my name like a prayer.
When I seeped back into my house,
no one knew who I was.
I thought I recognized myself
in the rooms I'd haunted,
but when I fell into my own bed,
beside my own wife,
I felt my skin stretching out,
trailing off for miles through the woods,
felt myself turning back into this dream river
where I wait each night for my daughter,
the exquisite arc of her casting,
the absolute hymn of the line slipping between her fingers,
and my wife standing on the bank calling
what used to be my name.

THE MAD ANGLER CONFESSES

I am the darkness in the basement,
the moisture dried up
in abandoned reels, nets tossed into heaps.
I am the boy with no shoes trying
to thrash his way out of the swamp of a three piece suit.
I am nothing more than a map of every
river left to fish,
every insect that hasn't hatched,
I am that singing sound of the fly line
you so want to hear miles from any river.
I am the deep pit
where the river you loved
vanished in a whirlpool of career moves,
the desperate murmur of talismans
forgotten in your heart.

THE MAD ANGLER IN THE CATHEDRAL

He spends a year removing the vaulted roof
fueled by the desire
to look up at night into a sanctuary of stars.
When he works, he speaks the names of ghosts, the liturgy of
entomology embedded in the dark water of his brain.
He believes in the gospel of intricate casts,
the psalms of mending line,
and drinking from the baptismal font, he prays
that all the angels might drift down, the sound of hymns
replaced by the singing of the fly lines they cast over the heads
of bait fishermen.

In the end, he tears down the walls,
channels a river through the pews,
and waits in the rain for the wild god of trout
to turn each swimming miracle loose from his hands.

THE EPIPHANY OF THE MAD ANGLER

When they called for my intellect I told them
it was dead, buried at the end of some worthless two-track
with a box of textbooks, then I walked to the river
to live among the fish,
and when they asked for my instincts I told them
that I traded them for the sense that rides on the surface
of the river, and knew instantly when I learned that the water of
rivers collects and eddies not in pools but in dark pockets of
wisdom, places under sweeping cedars where river stones have
arranged themselves into messages, a kind of braille,
places where the tongue of a man
wants to slide out of his head, swim away.

ADVICE OF THE MAD ANGLER

If you are miles from a river,
and you hear moving water,
have the sense to follow the woman next to
you out the door, into the woods,
where her body will slowly surround you,
the pure current of her flesh
smoothing you into that dark river stone
she will always carry in her pocket.

THE MAD ANGLER ON THE EXPRESSWAY

You would think, watching him,
that it was impossible to drive seventy
with a plow behind his truck,
but that's what he does,
his eight bottom discs
biting through concrete.
He stops at the bridges, pauses before he sets the charges,
then drives off, the plow churning behind him,
watching in the rearview mirror for another river that will
never be driven over again.
Later, he drives the abandoned two-tracks near his cabin,
stops to listen to the whisper
of the river he's headed for,
and that slight memory of exploding particles of
steel and asphalt settling like mayflies on the
ledger of every expressway river he's ever breached,
ever stream he has sanctified.

GOING NORTH

Going north means going
into something deeper than silence.
Mist hangs for hours in the woods
and the apparitions singing in dreams
know places we will never see.
You will know you are north
by the edges of the day
and the slight aura surrounding the trees.
Something in your muscles will be trying
to remember ancient directions,
the way into old hunting grounds,
and if you died
and someone threw your bones
into the water,
they would swim together
and form a long arrow
pointing north.

RIVER GODS

Sometimes they churn through rock,
then lie down in the beds
of the rivers they make,
their bodies still full of the sound of
moving water.

Sometimes they stop under the earth
and open their mouths
and those dark springs you see
in the forest begin to speak.

I have seen rivers turn countless times
and circle themselves,
I have seen rivers turn to ice overnight,
and rivers that come up out of their banks
and lie next to the bed,
and I have seen rivers leap into the veins of men,
their lives suddenly gone wild, misguided,
the river gods laughing somewhere
out in deep country
their hands brushing the earth
divining for water
as if it were blood.

DIVING FOR MY FATHER

for Dave Lemmen

It is 1958.
My father is lost
somewhere on Bass Lake.
I see myself grabbing at the water
over the side of the boat,
sure he is there,
floating face upward,
certain I will see
the glance of starlight off his eyes.
For a while I drag bottom
with a set of six treble hooks tied to a lead weight,
finally stopping in the middle,
the line fast at sixty feet.
I slide in,
take the line in my hands,
follow it down
to where he rests on the bottom,
both of us staring into the other's
blue eyes.
I put him on my back,
speak this dream into his ear,
and he tells me how he is there
nearly every night,
watching the stars
through sixty feet of clear water,
how it is that somehow
he enters my dream
through the bottom of the lake,
waits there to watch me
for the swimming down,
the carrying back.

OBA LAKE, ONTARIO

I am in a cabin halfway up the south side of Oba
Lake. It is one in the morning and the surface
of the water is perfectly smooth. Outside, when
I stand on the beach, I look up the lake, then
back down: twenty-two miles of smooth, black
water and the reflection of millions of stars.
The stars. I begin to lose my orientation and
think of the surface of the lake as another kind
of sky, a sky you might dip your hand into and
drink bits of galactic water, swallow hot
particles of star. Even better, I think to myself,
would be to drift out on the lake, the boat
pressed between two skies, two sets of stars.
How I might lean over the side of the boat and
swirl the stars into new constellations, or how I
might slip into the lake, swimming just under
the surface, the stars mixing with my skin.

Later, when I go in to sleep I keep thinking of
the stars. I dream stars, bits of stars caught in
the net of my dreams, my body turned to stars,
fishing in the starlight of my own body, pulling
huge pike up out of the belly of the lake, their
eyes glistening.

In the afternoon we fish the pockets, throw our
lures up close to the sheer rock cliffs. The pike
come out from under the ledges, their eyes
churning with old starlight, their bellies white,
sudden streaks against dark water. Just before
we sit down to eat the fish, I think of how their
bodies pulsed in my hands, how someone might
take each one of their scales from the cleaning
shed, walk to the lake in absolute darkness,

holding them clenched in one hand like bits of
silver, and how, when they fell, they might
resemble constellations, suns, bits of star sifting
out of a man's hand.

RIVER GHAZALS

1

All night I cruise bottom, my life an ice dream,
closed river mouths.

At the river she slipped down out of the air:
a woman with skin to be written on.

Not beside the river, but in the river,
rolling again and again toward deadfall.

The river's true heart: a cold spring under my flesh,
eyes blue as ice.

On the night river I trade my life for the lips of darkness.

2

Trade work for sleep. Trade sleep for hunger.
Give the hunger back to yourself.

The dog buried under the trees rises nightly,
carries a dream in her mouth.

A day of high clouds, the odor of honeysuckle
absorbed through her skin.

Dream dog, lick my wounds, take this body with you,
both of us drifting the river.

At the edge of the river a soul drops its kindling,
builds a small fire.

3

Three women slip out of the shadow of my life,
their lips brushing me like feathers.

A soul extinguishes itself, drifts toward the dark
	bottom where all loss comes to rest.

Always her voice: a river stone with a song inside,
or dying from the bones outward.

Suddenly, a man turns luminous, walks out of his life,
	gives himself to water.

4

There was a year of snow, dogs attacking the house,
silence frozen into muscle.

On the maps the weather raged.
Down below, I read the book of her skin.

An all day rain, the kind of rain that turns you shiftless
watching the empty road.

Let me love the humidity of her body,
the dark storm of her hair.

Watching the rain hit the river, eating brook trout,
rain in the fire, a life speaks back from the coals.

5

Think of your life as wind through a doorway.

Whenever you can, trade the bank for the river,
the sky for the bird, your skin for pure light.

Fuel your heart with single caresses, glances,
the sudden visions of your life gone feral.

Go to anyplace where there are more rivers than roads;
trade your flesh for any moving water.

Think of your life as a trigger, death in the target,
something blazing inside your chest.

6

Here, near the river, a day was lost, then another.
The heart turned inward, collapsing into a blister of pitch.

Yesterday the river was burnished by light, like brass.
I wanted to lie down, stretch molten sixty miles to the
      lake.

I walk the charred banks, the ghost dogs of friends coming
        up out of the ground. I try to weep them back to
           life in the river.

Each day I carry my body to the river, counting the
        bones.
Each day I count less, my body sifting away.

Pray to the water gods: no seams in your life.
A hand enters the river, disappears. A life in the current.

7

One last cast: a beautiful woman rises from the pool
        of sorrow
in my stomach. The full moon, clouds ripped apart in the
        wind.

Hold the darkest part of yourself over the water. Pray for
      sleep, a white water dream, the belly of the river
         against yours.

Just now, a brook trout slipping out of the mouth of a
        god.
The way light cuts through water, nations of stones.

I sat at the head of a sandbar covered with stones.
I stared, counted. Put it back together in a dream.

The body buried under the river: a mouth at last full of
    silence. A spirit rising like fog, the breath of the
        swamp.

8

Matthiessen alive on the River Styx. A great bird lifting off
    from under a shroud.

I gave my life away. Sent the skin to each compass point,
prayed that something still alive would drift back home.

All up and down the river: birds coming in to feed.
Inside my chest, my heart thinks it has wings, tries to fly.

What sound other than water can keep you alive?
Know the voice you choose to speak your name.

9

A river tattoo: on each arm another place to wish to die
    for. In the mirror I see my eyes rising like two moons
        over dark country.

In her sleep a daughter builds a raft. The perfect fit of her
    body against the single oar as she drifts away.

Upstream rain the river filling.
I walk home with the river aching in my legs.

I gave an eye to the river. Once a month the moon gives it
    back, then weeks of blindness, her body smelling like
        wet stones.

Her spine outlined against the last light on the river: a
    place between her breasts where water pools, cools
        the fever.

10

for Jim

23 years ago I read the ghazals for the first time,
and there near the river, something flew out of my skin.

Tonight, a full moon. I'm miles from where I need to be.
    All this living, then: moonlight down the hill moving
        like a river.

Carry your heart to the river. Pull the wings out from
    under your coat. Use your life like a talon, beak,
        tearing loose.

Get back: to swamps, to feeder-creeks that have no
    names, those places where your life turns and follows
        the current.

One river ends, falls out of the body. The shadow of a
    man turns upstream, never looks back.

11

The Theory and Practice of Rivers: each day goes by, the
    current boiling around the rock you have made of
        your life.

Asleep by the river a dream rises up off the bottom. Your
    chest cleaves, something with a heart made of water
        slides in.

Woman to be river, river to be flesh, night to last. You
    pray for a lifetime to be washed up against her.

In the knot of deadfall I saw how a life tangles, then how
    part of the body drifts off, collects downstream to heal itself.

Follow the tracks to their disappearing. Find the origin of
    all rivers where time is cutting herself into ever smaller pieces.

12

This morning: a dream of all the rivers I've found in dreams.
All day: The great pleasure of water lodged under the flesh.

He went crazy. Built a cabin far from friends, saved himself
    for countless trips into the interior. Made fires, read the
        coals.

Where the river flows into another river: your blood moving
    at the speed of light, body a miracle of confluences.

Take this down: one dream a week you must wake inside
    the heart of the river. Come back to tell it.

The story goes like this: he conjured himself into a river.
Lay prone for days, his eyes following a sea of stars.

13

for Dave

I shape my life to the weather. Twelve degrees and falling.
    Each cast curling into the wind, driving snow, the sun
        a dream.

How many times do I say the dead man's name to pull
    him back? How many times do I dip my hand into the
        river expecting a miracle?

I would bring him up into the light. Give him his old
    name back.
Build a fire, tell him to stay close, back to the wind.

On the Betsie I lift the bodies of salmon from the river,
    take them to the sand bar, read the maps of their skin.

In my own fire near the river mouth I see his eyes. My
　　　body tries to drift off, learn the topography of the river
　　　　　bottom.

Today, I wanted to forget my name, leave my life packed
　　　in this skin near the river, pass away from this place.
　　　　　Pass away.

A LAST POEM: THE DEATHS OF FATHERS

It will certainly concern itself with light,
the way the light appeared on the morning of each
    death:
liquid, yellowed, frayed at the edges.

It will have something about rivers,
something about the beauty
of the way the bank holds the water,
how firmness knows enough to let something by
once in a while,
knowing it will come back,
settle in again.

This last poem will have something about the body,
about the bodies of sons in the late afternoons
of their fathers' deaths:
how all of them felt as if a shadow
had rended itself from the flesh,
walked away, turned
and through the distance of haze, waved,
not a signal of leaving,
but one which said:

"I will wait somewhere here on this other side
for your life to gather enough speed to cross over,"

and bending, each father will leave a sign,
some mark in the dust.

DRIFTING THE COASTLINES

THE COAST OF NOWHERE

Thirteen miles inland from Lake Michigan I can still hear the sound of the Platte River running over shallow gravel, a voice so perfectly clear I hear it in every room of the house, the pulse of river, the memory of current loose in the walls. And tonight, walking the river mouth near the house, I look up into the high branches of the red pines and listen to the questions in the wind, the way they sift through the delicate needles thirty feet in the air and then seem to fall at my feet: one asks the way into the heart, another asks whether the god of rivers and lakes is sleeping inside my hands, and the third, the one I cannot answer, asks if another decade of walking this coastline will bring me answers.

Once in the house, I look down through almost a century of trees, then begin to take them inside slowly. I pack the red pines closest to my heart, then lift in the maples, the giant oaks, then the rocks scattered along the shore. I take in the coastline, the river where it enters the lake. Somewhere inside, this landscape comes back together, each tree where it belongs, and the sky: the way the sky looks from the deck, looking due south toward the peninsula, staring hard into that middle distance two miles out in the middle of Green Lake, that spot where nothing seems to happen, only empty space, watching from the coast of nowhere, I tell myself, a spot where I send the worst of everything to straighten itself out.

Tonight, when I fall asleep, I'll dream walk this inner coast and when I pass my hands close to the trees I know, run them over rocks and stumps, they will glow like embers, this place so close to nowhere, so close.

THE TEXT OF THE RIVER

1

Your blood tells you first. Maybe on a warm night in May your blood changes its course, comes from somewhere beyond your body, from the ground, or from that spring you first saw years ago in the woods. Water coming from an iron ring in a small clearing, and you looked . . . first in and then down—into a perfect dark circle of water like an eye, a dark pupil, and you feel this water entering your legs first, then sifting upward into your heart.

Now, you realize you've carried this river in your heart for years. The slight taste of iron, the smell of the underbelly of ten thousand years while the glacier moved down, traced the course of that other river, and now this river is inside you.

Call it memory, call it the way your hands cup the water to drink, call it the form your life has taken, how what you do each day shapes itself around the river in your heart, or call it by name . . . AuSable, River of Sand . . . and know that your pulse rides on the back of water, rides for miles through swamps and deadfall, and know that the words you speak come from the mouth of the river, that even your skin, your hair, your face, has river in it.

To get to the river all you need is to sit still, drop down, let your body remember the way the river moves: always by way of gradient, a falling from higher to lower, a way your body has of lengthening out, thinking itself loose in the river. Not as water, but as the way time might mix with water, in swirls, in small whirlpools, or in the long runs of riffles dropping into deep pools. And it never stops but keeps running, falling, moving, your life sifted and re-sifted, as though you were once whole, a man, flesh and blood. And now you begin to understand the thin film of river which holds you together. A life gone over to water, a river, each movement in your life a part of losing yourself, getting yourself back, your heart always lifting water from that first deep spring.

2

Deep in the heart, deeper than memory, deeper than any water, under the river, in the grey rain of another kind of sky, the god of fish spends his days pulling the new grey bodies of fish from his side. He brings them to his lips, infuses them with the colors he senses inside him—bright silvers, slight touches of blue, some of them full pinks, their backs dotted like rain, then raises them upward into the world, speaking their names: brook trout, brown, rainbow. He tells them that death is the water they part, that the river will hold them, take them home, into the heart once more; in my pulse, in the wash of my memory, in the dance of the river, in my own clear eyes.

3

How do I speak the name of gravel, the heart of water? How do I walk the river for miles and never lose myself? How do I let my body fall into the river and not turn away from the world? How do I sift the river for voices? How do I rise each day and smell the odor of cedar in my skin? How will I follow this river if the river is inside me? Where do I find the dark lips of the river to offer the ragged edges of my life for healing?

4

Rain to earth, a single cut along my arm. Blood drains into the river, the blood of memory, of loss, of fear and desire, gone downstream. What seeps in is wild, part fish, part plant, the real blood of gods who still live, gods who are rivers themselves, gods who move like water over the sur- face of my heart, gods who move beside you in the rivers you fish, the gods of rivers who come into the body riding the flesh of brook trout, and the intoxicant single god of the one true river where you give blood and take blood. This is the god who bleeds into you, who stands up every day and makes you move through your life, remembering rain, sleet, snow, the way each form of water falls, mixes, passes away.

5

I walk the till of the glacier: sand, gravel, silt, clay and stones, moving up sometimes into the hilly moraines where the ice front stood still. There are times when months pass, then I wake to the sound of ice melting, and hear again the way the river leaves behind what it means. I carry the stones of ten thousand years home, lay them down on the desk, sort and re-sort. I roll them in my fingers like dice, let them fall again and again, reading the pattern each time, looking for some kind of omen, a prophecy, reading them like braille, like religion.

RIVER: FINDING THE WAY NORTH

1

Even in the rain when the surface pales and becomes covered with wind ripples, you will never know this river. If you floated all the way down it, working your way in and out of the deadfall, you would not come to knowledge. A man standing next to any section of this river will swear he feels a vibration, senses some wild electricity working through his body. There are nights in mid-December when the moonlight glinting off the surface makes it look as though it were covered with fireflies. At times, in August, you can watch the river from a high bank and think it is bottomless. The clarity of the water pulls at you. You bend close to see your reflection, and, instead, see farther than you have ever seen before.

2   Fall Rain

The rain moves through the air in sheets, stripping and covering the bottom with every color of leaf. During a rain you fully realize there are two rivers here. There is a river of water moving for two hundred and forty miles and underneath it is a river of sand and gravel. In this distance the river turns back on itself thousands of times. A man standing at its mouth will know it has rained at the headwaters by the texture of the water. When the river is high after a rain it moves through places usually unseen. Its backwaters and false channels confuse even the best of guides. The man who rides the river in a thunderstorm will be working against more than weather. During a rain the river seems to speak to itself. It undulates slowly. It will weave back and forth through the roots of jack pine and cedar, spread its body over the banks, and lie in the deep grass calling you in.

3   The Leaving

The man and his wife stand on the riverbank. It is early May. The sun is shining. This time, she is leaving for good. They speak, and a distance grows out of their words. The man shuffles his feet and watches the river. Shadows move across the water. Between the man and woman the day unwinds. The river moves past them. When the car arrives they both walk to the house. There are few words. Finally the woman stiffens her face, dips toward him, and leaves. The man follows her to the car. After she leaves he does not go back inside. He returns to the river, sits down, and watches the water. Something inside him unwinds, trails for miles, and finally snaps. For weeks he will rise early, watch the river, and think that he hears her somewhere in the room. When summer comes he will spend long hours close to the river. He will feel his senses coming back. He will feel them flow and fill places he had forgotten. During the winter he will fall away from his friends. He will grow down into himself. He will learn that when everything else fails he will still be able to sit and watch the movement of the water. He will learn to trust the river for its constancy. For the rest of his life he will be able to close his eyes and see the river. And, late at night, when his sleep is empty and troubled, he will lie back, hear the sounds of water come from far back in his head, and feel his body settle into sleep.

4   Fog

You will come to what you swear must be the last bend in the river. There will be smells in your nostrils which go beyond description, mixtures of cedar and mud, and a deep musty odor you will mistake for the breath of a beautiful woman. This is fog you can dip your hands into, squeeze together, and come out with nothing. How strange, you think, not to see your hand at the end of your arm. You conjure up images of yourself going in, parting the fog just enough to slip through, finding that spot on the bank where you are sure she must be sitting. She is cupping her breasts in her hands as though once there you could replace the emptiness in your own hands with the soft directions you are positive must be printed on her chest.

5   Power

This river could kill you, but it won't. It will confuse you. When you think you are riding the flow east, you will really be going west. When you try to take a compass reading, you will be wrong. The river has changed directions so many times in the last hundred years that the sun becomes a mirage. The man who has lived or camped on its banks will tell you that sometimes, late at night, you will have a sudden urge, even in the coldest months of the year, to run to the river for a drink or to lie down on its bottom and make love. There is a power which makes you want to dive to the gut of the river, curl your fingers into the gravel, take a deep breath, and give yourself over.

6 Warning

If all sense of the river erodes away inside you, there will still be the over-powering sense of water. There will be many days when nothing will sat-isfy your thirst except river water. When you dip a cup and bring it to your mouth, you will come as close as you ever have to purity. When you drink, you feel the water move all the way through you. You will fall silent. Your eyes will stay on the river. Something inside you will drift into an invisible center and that sound you hear will be the sound of your own blood pulsing close to the river.

7 Second Warning

Leave the river. It will stay with you. Miles from its source you will notice the smell of cedar coming from under your skin. The river is like a medi-cine. The idea of the river packs in close to your life and stays with you as a form of protection. You will always be aware of its presence. In conver-sations you will suddenly feel your concentration break loose and gather around a particular bend in the river. The river has its own weather, its own sounds, its own way of working into the wells of your memory. The river is always open. It has no reasons. It moves in a shallow bed in the earth, moving like a woman who is always leaving one lover and going to another.

8 Mist

It is too easy to call the river mist an apparition. You can become lost eas-ily in this weather. All your senses will be distorted. You will think you have walked too far, missed a crucial landmark. Your voice will leave your body and make a path through the fog. If you lie down in the river and let your body float downstream, you will have a chance to get out. Birds of prey will appear overhead as fast moving, dark shadows. You will become so cold you will want to feel the pain of a talon in your neck. If you can still breathe, take in as much air as possible and let the mist become part of you.

9 Last Warning

This river will tumble through you. It will fill your eyes and stretch itself into beautiful passages inside your body. Everything will look clearer. Once the river enters you, there will be something inside your body which will never sleep. If you touch the river it will go around your hand, around your body if you let it. The man who has been close to the river in all seasons carries a special knowledge with him. He knows death is in the water, that it moves along beside the river like a shadow. This death is like a bridge from the river to that other place: the darker, tangled regions of the back country.

10 Back Country

Everything here is river. There are no banks or trees, only endless water flowing north. You will hear birds, but never see them. Fish will leave a flash of riled sand on the bottom. The weather here is a combination of all weather. The wind blows steadily and there is a slight October sharpness to the air. There is only one direction: north. This is where true north begins, where water acquires the taste of iron. There are no trees or swamps. Only water. Even if the earth fell apart, this place would still exist. There are no trails in, no marked waterways. There are no maps. Only stories.

11 Directions

I used to think in terms of pure direction, waiting for my skull bones to find the perfect alignment, the wind hooking around my neck, pulling me into the roots of my senses. Now, I want to sit down by the edge of the river and imagine I have lived in water since birth. I want to wake in the morning and feel water seeping out of my eyes, feel my heart dance and surge with every full moon. I want to say I know this river, safe in the knowledge that even in darkness I might use my mind as a kind of compass, the bones gone resonant, leading me through miles of wilderness.

12 A Story for Someone's Death

It goes this way: for weeks the old man lay in fever. His lips moved continuously, a voice coming from deep in his belly, asking for water. If he had been near the river, they should have carried him down so he could stretch his old arms full length in the icy water. The deep cracks of his skin would fill with the ointment of pure coldness, and later that night, troubled in a dream of the fire under his skin, he would wake to the taste of the river, the memory of the cold, the way his lips drank it in, the taste of iron turning to blood. He would hear his voice as he had known it before: rich and flowing, the sound of black ice mixing with the howl of the wind, his body cupping into itself, then driven upward, a spike of pure direction churning into white light, his body free and clean.

THE RIVER EVERYWHERE

For Claudia

1

Under the sky, under the bed, under the house, the most beautiful woman I have ever seen is stepping out of her skin, as if out of delicate silk. She holds her skin in her hands as if it were cloth and begins to wring it slowly, and slowly, the most beautiful water begins flowing. When she lifts this water up into this world, her hands cup toward my face and when I drink her, I know for the first time that her river is where I have lived my whole life.

2

Even before I realized it, a river was following me underground. When I slept, it stopped moving and stayed like a shadow under the bed. And when I fished, it coursed, just above bedrock. Once, I remember hearing this river, like a voice from a closet, or a cellar, a place where the husk of a life fell into itself and was saved by the breath of the river.

3

The river is running now over the desk, through my hands, running in the white threads of my shirt, moving in each molecule of my hair: Upstairs I hear my wife and daughter laughing while the current sifts past their bodies. When I go up the stairs they are both resting like stones on the floor, the river running translucent over them, like a second skin.

4

When my daughter falls asleep I hear the river running under her bed, a dream river now and I hear her building a raft in her dream and I want to stop her from pushing off. All night I hear her voice calling from downriver, trailing off. I slide toward her mother. Our love is water. I pray to whatever water god would trade the days I have left to turn our lives to water, so that in the instant our lives meet there will be no seam, no difference in the current of her body and the current of mine.

THE DREAM RIVERS

1

Lost again, this time on the Pere Marquette and up ahead the snow forms into the torso of someone you never had the chance to know. This is the place they'll find you in the spring: two legs dancing in the current, your neck tied with twenty-pound monofilament, one eye slightly askew, the grin on your face from a week of ecstasy, the way you imagined her torso to drape down over you like a shroud, how she moved with the motion of the river, and because she was made of snow, how her skin settled into your own.

2

You wash up in your sleep, your belly white, eyes opaque, like tiny moons floating in your skull. You love this ritual, this way all of the women in your life come to you with intentions of rescue, how they slip their hands under your head, letting the river pass over you. One of them whispers that all the rivers on earth were once rivers of blood and to live once meant finding that one true river, cutting yourself open, wading in, letting the river pass through, the women sifting into your eyes, your hair, your body like a river.

3

I see them sometimes, walking the banks when I fish, their arms raised in a half wave, their faces contorted. Even from the middle of the river I know on each face I see a little of my own, knowing that these ghosts are only husks, collections of bad dreams, lost places, remembrances of all the things I never was. Some are the spirits of relatives dead thirty years too soon, the ghosts of alcoholics, horse thieves, prisoners of war. For hours I have fished and seen them drift off bottom, their huge eyes blue and clear, then my life feels as if it separates. Half of me goes downstream fishing between deadfallen cedar, the other half slips in, lies down in familiar arms, goes back, wild, to the river.

4

One river falls out of the moon, the other begins in a photograph from the 20s. Hemingway up in Michigan, stepping off a boxcar, the flare strapped like an antennae to his pack, headed north, tramping the streams, each twist of his wrist, each cast arcing toward that last day in Idaho when the shotgun lay in his hands, the barrel icy, a thousand rivers releasing all at once.

5

Once, on the Platte, the moon, stars, reflected in a cup of whiskey, the mirror image of one eye looking through itself, like peering in the front of a pinhole camera. Only you look back, see your father casting before you were born. The line moves away from him like light, and you feel that pull, how he baptized you with a handful of river water when you were eight years old, gave the first drink and then drank himself, and each movement now is a memory of how the river moved that night, how your father has river in him, how your river is the same as your father's.

6

Maps turn red, rivers turn to blood. A body stands, is part map: the ghosts of rivers haunt the veins, casting under half moons, knowing there are fish struggling out of the heart.

7

"Water will never leave earth" you wrote, and tonight I send what little is left of my spirit toward that black feeder-creek near the house, then sit down back inside and watch, waiting for its return, thinking how my spirit will look when it comes in the back door, holding a woman made entirely of water, thinking how my spirit would enter this woman, run the darker regions inside her, ride the current of her wildness home.

THE RIVER INSIDE

1

Weeks go by, then months, the river iced over. There's no particular place to walk, and each trail to the river is covered again by the time I walk back to the house. Each night before I go to bed I walk to the edge of where I think the bank and the river come together. I lie down with my ear pressed against the ice, listening: This deep vein of water rises north of me, comes down through cedar swamps and meadows, the clear gravel riffles near Grayling. I think to myself on this ten-below night that there isn't a voice down there, only an echo. I'm tempted to tell myself I hear things in the current, or sense, in the slow rising of bubbles trapped against ice, that I recognize the message. But there is no message. No voice here in the night coming from the belly of the river. This is the kind of night when anchor ice is born, when the river stiffens. Weeks from now, when the spring rains come, what's left will sweep the river clean, the ice cutting through deadfall, moving rocks for miles downriver. In August, if you're lucky, you can bend down into a pool and find a piece of river shale marked and cut, a kind of sign language left as a reminder that there is no time, no day or week, no month, no full moon, no new moon. Only the slow, constant motion of water and ice, the heave of seasons, the river's long life only getting longer.

2

Back low in the trees the full moon is gathering itself to lift over my head. Upstream the river has the broken castings of moonpath, the dimples of hundreds of tiny fish rising. In the swamp, my body turns away from the world, away from roads. I sit under the sweepers of a hundred-year-old cedar, and watch night sift in from the marsh. A nighthawk sluices downriver, the deep "vrooo" of its voice a perfect language for the way the sky and the river switch places. When I stand to speak into the woods I say only my name. I say who I am into the dark and nothing comes back. I wait after each telling and then turn my name into a question. What I hear is only current, the way water deflects from deadfall, a way silence has of catching in the throat. What good comes of this repeated calling, this sending out of my name? This silence? Hours later when I slide into bed, I think I hear something like I have never heard coming from my lips: a voice like darkness itself, the words rising from my belly, filling the room with something dark and empty as if I were calling back through forty years, my lips alive with whatever it was I had lost.

3 X

For days now I have come to the river without fishing on my mind, seeking only the way the current takes things away. I drop bits of leaves, pine needles into the river and watch them head downstream. I put my hand in and watch it vanish, then my arm and shoulders and suddenly I am sliding my torso toward bottom, only my head holding in the wash of the Platte. Underwater, my eyes dissolve away, the sun only a memory, the smell of river intensified in whatever it is that I have let myself become. Somewhere downstream under a logjam, under roots, in a bed of gravel, my body comes back to itself, rising up through cool morning air. I carry this sense home: water sifting through rock, through skin, through bone, through memory. Water taking the mind away from itself as if the hands of water could sort and cleanse, and then turn the self loose back into the world. Tonight, walking the hills near the house, I lift my hands to my face and taste the river on my fingers, some small part of me miles away, sidling back and forth in the current, darkness just now settling over the river.

4 X

Under the bridge I watch the salmon roll and spawn. Later, downstream, I take a drink of death water, my lips falling away. All up and down the river, birds coming in to feed. Inside my chest, my heart thinks it has wings, tries to fly. I speak my own name into the shifting light of an October afternoon, send it out over the water. I speak the names of fish, the birds, all the plants I know. I try to lift off from this place, but my feet won't leave the edge of the river. I squat down near a sandbar and try to memorize the way the rocks have been nudged into place, each stone a marker, a leaving, some way the river has of keeping track of its past. Two old salmon sweep by, their bodies dark and mottled. They move upstream, death riding on their backs. A female rolls toward the male next to her. On the surface of the river I see the reflections of bright maples, and there, in that other world underwater, I watch them spawn, then drift back downriver. I think of how the afternoon gathers itself, how it is that a man can come to the edge of a river and watch death swim by, then go home to make love, or merely look out the window long enough to see himself struggling to get the rider away from his life. And in his sleep he knows the river is moving, the salmon are rolling. Creatures are being ridden to exhaustion.

5

All night I have wandered the woods, headed deeper into the Dead-stream. At the river's edge I trace the path of the moon as far upriver as I can see. Mayflies drop out of the air, the surface of the river dimpled with thousands of dying flies. I cast upstream, follow the drift, mending line, always mending. In the semi-dark, in the moonlight, I think I see the out-line of my own body as it steps from under the darker arms of cedar sweepers. I stand perfectly still and when it passes directly in front of me, I hear it whisper: "Think of what is left of your life as the water that is passing in front of you right now." I step back on the bank and watch myself trail downriver, then take off my clothes and swim upstream, my mouth gathering in as much water as possible, moonlight, the wash of river. Wounds I thought I had forgotten suddenly heal, something inside my life gathers itself, turns further inward, lets the river pass through.

6

Today, high clouds being torn apart in the wind. Each time I come home from the river I feel the precipitate of walking upstream, sitting at the smallest of waterfalls where a feeder-creek feeds into the Platte. I leave stones there every time, tiny markers, one or two placed in the wash of cold spring water. This afternoon, walking up the drive to get the mail, I took a river stone from my pocket, thought of how it was formed by heat and pressure in a time almost before time. Back inside, I put the stone back in the tiny river I have made on top of my desk, each stone perfect, each one a reminder of the message of what was left behind. Tonight, just before I fall asleep, I'll watch this little river like I watch the real one, sure there are fish in every pool, something alive in the trees and deadfall. And when sleep comes I'll carry stones back to the dream river, put them back where they belong.

7

When I wake in the middle of the night I listen for the river, the hiss of rain again, the memory there in the dark of another language I thought I had forgotten. In almost pitch black I hunch down by what's left of the fire, stir the hot ash with a piece of pine kindling. What catches fire comes like a word out of the ground, sifting up through the trees, moving slowly away from this place where I have come to forget what I know, forget my own face, my skin, the way I speak. I taste the ashes, carry the voice of embers back to the tent. Before I fall back to sleep I taste the burnt pitch on my tongue. I think of new words for trees, the sky, the way my life has hung in some odd kind of balance all these years. And I think of how the river moves past this camp in the dark, this place where a man is just now struggling to speak something he does not know.

WADING THE
DARKER CURRENT

OUT FOR BLOOD

There is the strain of sitting in the fighting chair of a large ocean craft, strapped into a fishing harness, a kind of mini-straightjacket, your arms turned to jelly against a huge marlin. And there is the contrasting joy sitting in a rowboat, drinking beer and casting plugs for bass under a full moon. But there is something about salmon fishing that takes you into the realms of philosophy and religion: standing chest deep in a river watching the movements of hundreds of fish, all on their spawning run upstream where they will mate and eventually die. And you're out there, standing in a river that is at once alive and surging with fish and again is like standing in water that flows directly from the mouth of death.

Give me September and October off work and a supply of hard currency and I'd head for certain points on the globe where salmon fishing is at it's most refined: Iceland, Nova Scotia, New Brunswick, but above all, Scotland. I'd spend lots of cash to fish in Scotland, on the Spey River where you can rent a section of river called a "beat" and fish under the watchful eye of a ghillie, or guide, and hook salmon after salmon. And at night, back at the inn, you have your fish cooked for you, all the while sipping whiskey that you swear has boiled up from the ground itself.

Salmon fishing in such exquisite places as Scotland is done under ritualistic, prescribed conditions. There are rules and expectations set forth by your fellow anglers. You have to know how to act and you have to act according to very old traditions handed down by generations of fishermen. And if you've caught the legendary fish that your ghillie has told you has hung under the bank for a decade or so, then you become the legend itself. After you leave, your name will sift through conversations for years. Reverence. A kindly Scottish nod toward all the skill and patience you so aptly displayed.

In Scotland you're not out for meat, necessarily, but to honor the tradition of salmon fishing and its sport, often using expensive, hand-made two-handed bamboo fly rods, equally expensive reels, all the while dressed to the hilt with an oiled cotton jacket and a tie, of all things. But there are other places in the world where you come to find that the word "beat" takes on literal interpretations, particularly when it comes to salmon fishing in northern Michigan.

If you are about to go salmon fishing in northern Michigan, forget any pastoral notions of fishing, forget Scotland and all its finesse. Forget the modicum of civility you found on the chalk streams of England or the blue-ribbon rivers of New England. Northern Michigan salmon fishing is the equivalent of electroshock therapy. And for the purposes of analogy, salmon fishing in other areas of the world, particularly Scotland, is like being hooked up to the electrodes by a woman of refinement, say Beverly Sills, the wondrous opera singer, while up here, our kind of fishing, north of the forty-fifth parallel, is more akin to having Madonna jump start you with a car battery.

What we're talking about here is fishing for blood, meat, salmon that have come from the water of Lake Michigan to spawn and die, but not before you've had your chance at them.

And forget the good life on the way over. There are no stops for caviar or cognac in crystal snifters. At best, if you stop at Johnnie's Log Cabin Bar outside of Honor you can get a draft and a shot of Yukon Jack, then sift through the smoke for a woman to whet your appetite for fishing. And you'll likely find her: large, robust, a local, the kind of woman who would gladly cradle your head between her thighs and then crack it like an egg.

This is beer territory. A place where a college degree is a serious liability. A region of the upper Midwest where you are probably surrounded by all kinds of outlaws, poachers, lumberjacks on the lam, and more con men than on any corner in New York. It's desperate here, and so is this kind of fishing.

Even before you get to the river you need to get your head ready to face a veritable gauntlet: men, most of them drunk and too many from out of state, who have loaded themselves up with flagons of alcohol and the most crass equipment possible. Normally you would fish for salmon with an exquisite bamboo fly rod, a hand-tied salmon fly, and a head full of reverence for the angling tradition you're about to enter. Not so on the salmon streams here.

Your first reaction after pulling onto the shoulder to park is that you'll need some kind of weapon to fight through the crowds. And you're dead right. There are lots of out-of-state plates, vans, big four-wheelers with coffee mugs on the dashboards driven by the locally unemployed. Your first step into the swamp path back to the stream puts you headed for trouble.

At the river you'll likely meet up with large groups of drunken tourists-come-fishermen disguised as natives, many from such unlikely places as Georgia or Louisiana, where they haven't ever seen a salmon.

From here, the vision of lots of men stomping up and down along the river gets worse.

There's no room here for high-dollar equipment, delicate rods, oiled cotton jackets, or sporty hats. These guys mean business. They fish, not with flies, which are the legal means of hooking fish, but with large and illegal treble hooks, three nasty pitch-fork-looking contraptions wired together, twenty-pound monofilament line, and brutishly thick rods that most of them use at home to pull their engines and transmissions.

Their methods are equally brutal: they don't cast and retrieve, cast and retrieve, the usual method of putting the lure to the fish, working the fly with the deft touch of a magician—an act of meditation. Instead, what they do with their treble hooks tied to lead weights the size of small anchors is more akin to dredging. Similar, I would say, to the way the Coast Guard drags for bodies. They usually cast up above the salmon pools and then rip down through the bottoms of them, often foul hooking fish and then hauling them up on the bank. Great sport for city dwellers and those with football-score I.Q.s, most of whom have driven for hours in search of easy meat, not sentiment and reflection, the nether side of fishing.

At other sites along the river the story is the same. When you step into the line of over a hundred men along the bank and begin casting, you've essentially said you're in for the duration. If someone hooks a fish and says "Fish-On" then everyone takes their line out of the water, the fisherman walks past, lands his fish and then immediately walks back to the spot he held before he caught the fish. Pecking order. Pissing order. If you get in someone's spot, you pay.

I have seen men driven up against their cars by other fishermen wielding tire irons all because they stepped into the wrong spot in line. And I have seen men bloody each other over hooked fish and I have seen men chase salmon out of the water and up onto dry land, then gaff them for the broiling pan.

My own tastes, largely fed by years of fly fishing for trout, a more delicate art, have me on the stream when almost everyone is either too drunk too continue, or exhausted from keelhauling so much meat on a given day. For me, fishing is a pursuit steeped in ritual and reflection. Robert Traver, perhaps the finest of angling writers, once wrote that his fishing was "an endless source of delight and an act of small rebellion." Quite simply, I fish because it takes me into a world where I am the predator. Even though I mostly practice catch-and-release fishing I honor the practice of taking game or wild food from the environs where I live. The poet Gary Snyder invokes this necessity as a way to keep some sense of the wild in ourselves. And wild, I feel, when I am fishing alone.

I often stand in the failing light and wait for a salmon pool to fill with spawning fish. I have seen four or five hundred at a time in a pool the size of an old De Soto. Most evenings I'll cast a delicate nymph pattern and let in drift along the bottom, waiting for the strike at the end of the drift. Then the slight lift and the fish is hooked.

The reel hums and vibrates and the hooked salmon moves like lightning in this small stream. I'll fight the fish for ten or fifteen minutes and then bring it to my hand, exhausted. For an instant there is that predatory instinct and I dispatch the fish, as they say, with a "priest," really a darkly polished walnut club handed down from generations of fisherman. After that, I watch the fish fade, first from bright silver to a dull grey.

Once a year I go into the swamp alone. I fish all night. And I remember a few things. I remember that in front of this very pool I am fishing I have watched men haul up salmon like old boots, beat them and rise from the banks with their hands bloody, and then another pass of their hooks and they are at it again.

When I hook my last fish I bring him into the gentle arc of lantern light. Pure silver pulsing, spent there in the dark. And just before I begin to clean him I think of those old photos of the salmon ritual from the Northwest Indian tribes: the chief wearing a suit made entirely out of salmon skins. The bounty of salmon nourishing a tribe, an entire way of life, right thinking. Even though the fish dies quickly, it still quivers there in my hands, its nerves flashing like distant stars.

Then I begin the same ritual I have followed for years. No chants, but the awareness that I am about to extinguish the life of a fish to enrich my own: one cut and I find the heart. Tiny. Glistening there in my hand like a large ruby. And every fall I eat the raw heart of one salmon, then I cook the fish in the coal of the fire. Call it ritual. Call it a need to eat something entirely wild. Call it an act of desperation, but there is something in the heart of salmon that asks death to wait a little longer at the door. And there is something equally insistent that eating this fish alone in the dark of the swamp, far from the supermarket, far from shrink-wrapped, force-fed meat, arranged like rows of shoes, is, finally, a way to keep the soul engines running on spirit rather than commerce and cash.

On the way home I pass the vans still parked on the road. Quiet now, most of the men asleep, passed out, the smell of fish and beer and piss mixed in the bushes. All the way home I feel the ache in my arm of casting, hooking fish, a night of salmon exhaustion in my forearm. And I feel each beat of my heart. Steady. Rhythmic. A man with two hearts, one his own, the other: salmon. And all the way home I dream myself into a suit made entirely of salmon skins and I feel a new pulse: how the wild salmon heart hammers inside my chest while my own heart cups the blow.

THE LEGACY OF WORMS

To a fly fisherman who has an inflated opinion of himself and his frater-
nity, nothing is quite as loathsome as a worm fisherman. Perhaps, because
of the media attention over the years to the "purity" of fly fishing, worm-
ing has gotten some bad ink. I must confess to a certain snobbishness at
times. After all, who am I kidding when I step into the AuSable with a
thousand dollars worth of Orvis gear? I'm fishing. I'm worthy of practic-
ing deception. I've got the stuff to prove it: fly boxes, graphite rods, tiny
gadgets with the right logo. But this is all fakery. We all know, when we
drool over equipment, that somehow, beyond this world of high-tech
boron-graphite fibers, underneath all this foppery, there is instinct.

Maybe it was instinct that told me to get up early with my father to go
looking for worms. He knew the best places: under leaves, cool and moist.
Or we went out late at night on the summer lawn, feeling in the dark for
crawlers, remembering later how they slipped like greased sausages
through our fingers. Even now, from a distance of thirty years, I can still
hear the sound they made when they plunked into the wet leaves and dirt
at the bottom of a rusty Hills Brothers worm can.

If fishing is about anything for me, it is about recollection, the way
my mind has of letting itself unravel and hook around the sensation that
the dead are surely watching us from the banks or are standing on shore
measuring each cast. Inevitably, when I think of ancestors and fishing I go
back to Bass Lake and my grandfather's cottage. I go back to fishing with
live bait, almost always worms—any kind of worm we could find. Back
then, in the fifties, I learned the secret techniques from my father and
grandfather about how to think of the hook as a kind of needle, the worm
as fabric, the whole rig set up to keep the worm alive as long as possible,
moving, imagining its slow dance underwater.

And the ghosts are always there when I fish now. I can see my grand-
father baiting up for perch using tiny red worms, or my father and me
anchored just off a deserted island, how we sifted through the can of
crawlers for the patriarch of all worms, the one that felt lucky. Then he'd
break one in half and spit on it and I'd make that long cast toward the lily
pads, waiting for the bass to explode up out of the weeds.

There are other visions, some taken from my father's stories, and
always they are visions of ritualistic, nearly sacred value: men hunched
over hooks in the rain, mumbling old fishing prayers, invocations carried

on the souls of countless worms. But the most stunning image is one passed on about one of my father's old fishing buddies from the forties, Fred Lewis, and how he must have looked when he turned toward a question just after baiting up, the hook in his teeth, and a gob of nightcrawlers dribbling down the side of his mouth.

Now, each year, maybe out of respect for the dead, maybe out of superstition, before I set my gear up, before I get out my hundred-and-fifty-dollar fly reels, the flashy graphite rods, the Wheatley fly boxes, I go into my study and take out the bandana in which I have wrapped the talismans of my life. A power stone from Lake Superior is hidden in there, and a lovely handmade Chinese fish given as a gift by an equally lovely student. Perhaps most powerful of all, there are bits and pieces of what's left from my grandfather's tackle: misshapen sinkers, rusted hooks, used crawler harnesses, the stuff of fishing a lifetime with worms. What was handed down from his gear as legacy has all been blessed: blessed by the blood of fish, blessed by the way his hands used these simple fishing artifacts, blessed by his patience and by his knowledge of the fundamental necessities of fishing.

STEELHEAD DREAMS

Tonight, just before I fall asleep, I hear the wind kick up in the red pines outside the house. I begin to go under, begin to submerge myself in a dream I know is waiting for me. "The steelhead run with the wind," I remember someone saying. And I think of thousands of fish gathering at the mouths of rivers up and down Lake Michigan. I begin to think of my bed and how I lie on top of it as some way I am able to hover just over the dream. As if the dream itself were made of water and I could lower myself down into a river choked with March ice. Holding. Just off a river mouth.

I listen. Underwater the wind sounds like thousands of waterfalls. A dull roar. A roar coming from far off and seeping gradually into my head. There are hundreds of fish waiting. They fan slowly, move up and down, some sideways in the current coming out of the river.

If I listen clearly enough to the inside of my head, I can hear the sound of some old command, some old memory let loose far upstream calling me in.

The water turns chemical. Chemicals loose in the tiny brains of these fish washing through their bodies, urging them upriver.

They surge through deadfall, upstream, rounding bends deep underwater, the sound of the river mixing with the sound of wind. All chemical. Something drifting now in their bodies. Bodies that look like pure aluminum muscles loose in the water.

First light. The fish stop just below the dam. The water moves past their eyes boiling with ice. In the steelhead dream I drift just off bottom. The bed, mattress, the room gone icy. I think I hear echoes in my head. The sound of rocks moving underwater. Fish moving against each other. Each fish noses into the current, settling toward bottom. My arms and wrists go limp in the dream, only a few hours left to rest here. Hold close to bottom. Pretend I know the way back. Pretend I can somehow rise back into my body, barely able to lift myself toward sunrise.

The fishermen move out of their houses hours before dawn. Maybe the river is twenty, thirty miles away. Or maybe they come from the cities, drive all night, migrating north.

In their cars, their heads begin to turn to steel. They imagine their arms and legs slowly churning to the color of slate blue. Their eyesight narrows. Their cars begin to swim through the darkness and when they stop to rest and step out into the night they believe the stars are the tiny points of hooks. They move farther north, not by watching the constellations, but by following the magnetic pull of steel forming in their heads. In their brains the cells are vibrating in close time with rivers. So close they hardly notice their bodies turning silver, their muscles taut, eyes running against the current of darkness flowing up over their hoods.

I send the line out thirty feet. "Steelhead run with the wind," Driscoll tells me. It drifts down the chute formed by the dam. I feel the lead weight bounce over gravel for twenty, perhaps thirty yards. Three minutes in the water and my feet go numb. Ice forms on my rod tip. I pull back slowly, hoping for a slight resistance, the mouth of a steelhead nosing my fly. Nothing.

Driscoll casts into the current. In four years, he has landed over three hundred steelhead. He tells me he fishes steelhead because if gives him some kind of balance. Fishing, he tells me, particularly steelhead fishing, has nothing to do with thinking. It is the balance between the cerebral, the meditative, and the physical. The biggest thing, he says, is the directness with which you catch a steelhead.

I have fished for trout for years. Never for steelhead. Mostly alone. Mostly in the early morning. Streamers laid out, then retrieved slowly. Meditative. Now, there are men upstream and down. Close. Packed in like fish. I cast perhaps forty times. Nothing.

Downstream men bunch together over the holes. They cast into the growing light. Suddenly, back near the dam a steelhead plunges upstream.

Someone's rod bends toward the water. The fish surges back downstream, then turns sideways against the current. The man holds. We pull our lines in. Everyone watches as he walks past us, holding the rod in close, bent almost double.

In the current the fish looks like a silver missile ripping upstream. Twenty minutes later he walks by, holding thirty inches of pure silver muscle, his fingers hooked under the gills.

He puts the fish on the stringer, ties it to an access fence pole, then goes back to fishing. I watch the fish fan slowly in shallow water.

We head home empty. I remember what Driscoll says about this sport. It's all in the drift, the length of your lead, the test line you use, and the weight and placement of split shot, he says. He tells me to walk the rivers, find out, he says, where the fish are and aren't, and then figure out why they aren't.

We go out another night. Fish the "rope hole" on the Platte River out of an old duck-hunting canoe. Forty degrees and raining/snowing, the wind ripping into my parka. "Steelhead run with the wind," he says again. We break several lines, casting again and again under the influence of mercury vapor lights from nearby cabins. Nothing.

I begin to think about this kind of fishing. Begin to think of the sheer number of fishermen standing next to each other at the Homestead Dam, and the sport turns narcotic. I begin to realize that the steelhead is in the brain. It runs deep, cuts down through the medulla, cerebellum, runs like a vein directly down the spinal column.

We leave again with nothing. On the way home I imagine the road to be a kind of river. I am guiding the truck directly into driving rain and snow. Both of us sit encased in steel. Steelhead fishermen. Driving home. Empty. Behind us the steelhead surge and circle at the river mouth. The truck fishtails through slush. A truck of steel. Heads of steel. And on the hood: ice clinging to steel.

FISHING THE WINTER RIVER

There are no tracks down to the river. Not any human tracks anyway. The woods have that stillness they hold all winter: in this relatively warm winter air sound is muffled enough so that when you speak a word, perhaps your own name, it hangs only inches from your mouth then dies quickly. In colder weather I have heard traffic from M-72, three miles away, sounding as if it were on top of me.

My second thought isn't of the weighted nymphs I'll use or how heavy a tippet to fish for a perfect dead drift. I think of June. Late June and this same stretch of water alive with Brown Drakes. I've fished where I'm standing so many times I know I could fish it blind. I fished a score of Sunday mornings up under the sweeping arms of cedars, streamers before dawn. I aimed for the dark pools, the browns looking for one more brook trout before the sun cracked the tree line. And one particular day in mid-August when it was almost a hundred degrees and no air. I left a friend's cabin, sweating profusely in the twenty steps down to the river then cast lackadaisically to no fish until I put a grasshopper up under a hanging cedar, dropping it just at the mouth of a small feeder-creek. What followed was fifteen minutes of thrashing around in the heat with an eighteen-inch rainbow. Dead luck. Dead hot.

But today, of course, I feel the cold even in my teeth. I feel like something dressed not for this world but for a Martian night, moving stiffly like a kid bundled up for an hour of snowman-making. At the end of my line the nymph hangs from the slightest tippet: almost unworldly in this world of absolute clarity. The river is as clear as . . . well . . . as ice. And I imagine to myself that this isn't water I'm fishing but some form of liquid ice, or the inside of a child's Christmas snow scene. I'm in the crystal ball and the snow is falling like feathers.

Perhaps because of the way the light slants this time of year, or perhaps because of the particular pensive slant of my imagination, I drift between the literal world of the river in front of me and the other world of the river I have in my head. On the winter river, as I see it today, everything looks clearer, somehow closer. I remind myself that what I'm walking is really the till of the glacier. An odd thought that I'm fishing in the belly wash of the last gasp of the ice age.

I remind myself, looking up toward the white ridge along the river, that the rocks at my feet slipped slowly out of the glacier and may not have moved far over the last ten thousand years. I slow my pace, lift a few pebbles from the bottom, knowing that sometime in the dead cold of February I'll take them out, lay them on the desk and sort and resort, put them in my mouth and taste: glacier, a hint of iron.

With the stones absorbing body heat in my pocket, I cast a summer cast, or a late fall cast, thinking again of the time I floated through here in a riverboat with the lightning dancing overhead and suddenly I remember to slow down. December fishing rhythm is slower, steadier, more measured . . . a way of keeping yourself warm as well as a method of delivering a fly. Fishing the winter river seems more meditative. With no intrusion from the human world, the mind has a way of opening up, even though the cold is knocking at the door of the warmest parts of your interior. So, meditative and cold, as if I were in some Japanese print, I move slowly, like the way ice moves downriver.

The water I'm moving through is as haunted as any I know. For over twenty years I've left parts of myself here, first as a resident and now as a visitor. In fact, just downstream there's a stump I call the "quarter hole": once in a moment of absolute boredom when a Hendrickson hatch didn't happen I slipped a quarter into the deeply decayed fracture of an old cedar. Now, I do it every time I pass through, the quarters giving off a soft glint, a silver matte patina etched by the daily abuse of the weather.

Back in the real world, the snow makes the river clearer in my head, the water mirroring a grey sky. I think of the river, the sky, the other interior river I carry inside me and tend carefully in my imagination: a dream river where all loss and despair disappear. A dream river where all the rivers of my life merge into one, while back on this river everything seems to have gone into this perfect greyness, and I become lost in the grey of the river. If I could, I would trade my life, right here, right now, for a life on the river, let myself dissolve into the snow I see up ahead as the river literally vanishes downstream. "Where'd he go?" someone might ask at the bar. "Just disappeared once." Into the cold. Into the grey. Into the dream river.

So I move slowly downstream, half imagining, half dreaming the nymph at the bottom of pools, suspended like something frozen in ice. I think of its tiny humped body washing in currents I can't see, the wing case only slightly bulging, if at all. And then I think of the magnitude of fishing: this river, all this water and a single dark nymph swimming across the pool in front of me. And I think of the fish: just beginning to settle in to a winter of slower metabolism. Their tiny brains hazing over with the onset of months and months of snow, wind. Sleet. The constant freeze and the occasional thaw, the sun mostly a thin, ghostly disc in the sky. It's the fish I think of late at night all winter, how they hover, barely moving for hours, pacing themselves, their bodies rippling against the slow crush of icy water.

Right now, getting colder, I mull over my casting options as I stand above a pool, where in July, I catch fish on the surface. Instead, I know they're deep. Sulking, turning slowly every so often to take in a winter nymph. If you were down there with them, watching their eyes, their fins, you'd know that they move ever so slowly, economizing, hunkered down in the dark December water, almost oblivious to any form of casting. The list of procedures is short: a cast back upstream for a dead-drift, the Crosfield Pull or the Leisenring-Lift technique, none of which I'm even remotely familiar with, on the loose from the study and the books, adrift here in the grey dream. I opt for a fourth move: the swimming nymph swing, though I doubt anything, fish or nymph, is capable of swimming in this weather.

I cast and drift, cast and drift, letting the dark nymph swim ever so slowly, wading past places I knew. Places I know now are more important to me than my own backyard. Just below Pine Road I head into the stretch of water where I used to spend almost every summer night. I smell the odor of the winter river now. The fresh scent of snow. The odor of cedar and iron. Swamp gas. And I smell, as I did three springs ago, the acrid smell of fire. Up the bank I can still see the blackened trunks of trees, the swaths left by the rage of forest fire. For an instant, wading between the charred banks, I think I see the ghost dogs of friends, killed by smoke and flames, rise up out of the snow, their bodies whole, black again. I want them to leap into the river, but they drift over me and land on the other charred shore, vanishing into the woods.

I stopped fishing. Tried to start again, worked and fought with the idea of the dogs coming back to life in my head and then felt my heart sink, cold and heavy. I gave in and then headed for the truck. Walking back along the high bank past the water I had just fished, I realized that I had come up empty. No strikes. No fish. Nothing but chapped hands, throbbing knees, the cold deep inside me now. Somehow, that was the way it was supposed to be: destined when I left Interlochen, the leather book of weighted nymphs in the warmth of a fishing vest, my head awash with the smell of my wife's skin, the warm touch of a daughter's goodbye kiss, and the humid, wondrous odor of my golden retriever. The warmth of home.

I reminded myself of the great joy of fishing, even in the cold, even when your hands froze around the butt of a rod and you had to suck on the line guides to free them up, the small dots of ice drifting in your mouth, almost like small nymphs of pure ice. Suddenly, I was struck by opposing forces of desire: I wanted to go home and I wanted to stay on the river.

I wanted the ghosts of the fire-dogs to come back, their coats black and glistening in the healing water of the river. I wanted them to slide up to me in the current, whole again. I wanted the jackpine suddenly to turn green and I wanted to look downriver once more and see the iris beds in full bloom, the damselflies moving like small, dark clouds.

I wanted to hole up and build a small fire, warm my hands and face enough to want to get back into the water. In the last light of a perfect December afternoon I wanted to slip back into the river, fish just one more bend. I wanted to feel the slight touch of a delicate trout mouth, its jaws turning a nymph over and over. And then I wanted to disappear, live like a dog along the river so that I could come home and say that I had given myself over to water, to the elements, that I had rolled the stones and come up wild and above all, that I had wintered over.

THE LAST GOOD WATER

For Dan Gerber

I don't want to speak it, because in the telling I did not want it to vanish.

For almost all my adult life I have felt what Norman McClean described as being haunted by waters. It's no secret that river fish living in fast currents are altered by the water moving so swiftly past them. If water can cut the Grand Canyon, then it can sculpt the very cells in flesh. In the same way, my imagination has been shaped and honed by the rivers I fish, a lifetime of offering myself to the power of hydrology. Added together, all my fishing outings are no more remarkable than the next man's, except for a period of time in 1982 when my life seemed almost luminous.

I was traveling by foot part of that summer, traversing sections of the upper Manistee I had never fished. Weeks before my trip I studied topographical maps as if they were sacred texts, poring over declinations and elevations, trying to locate even the faintest of logging roads, or old game trails that might take me in to the more remote parts of the river. I daydreamed about what it might be like to shed the skin of my life, to go aboriginal, a walkabout in the northern Michigan sense: a man wandering the darker, tangled regions of a river system that still held bears and bobcats. I imagined finding arrowheads or scraping tools along the high banks of the river, camped by myself in old, stands of white pine, my hands sifting through the humus left by decades of fallen pine needles.

Of course, I fished. I spent hours, sometimes days, on individual bends, the river speaking in the constant tongue of water over gravel. For two weeks I managed to see almost no one. If I heard voices, I slipped out of the river and into the underbrush. Through the shafts of rushes and wild grass I watched the faces of strangers nymphing the river, listening to the way their reels clicked and spun. I hovered near the soft edges of their conversations, never wishing to enter into any dialogue. If it had been possible, I would have turned to stone or lichen, anything other than what I was. I needed some time to jettison a stalled career, and to reconcile the collected debris of a lifetime of teaching.

Sometimes, in the daylight, I held my arms to the river, my skin an etching of the current and it seemed as though I had begun to change into water. When I looked at the surface at the right angle I could see how mottled my face had become, those current-blown lines in the bottom sand beginning to appear around my eyes. If I died on the river I wanted someone to think he found the face of a great Indian warrior ala Edward S. Curtis, rather than a pasty-faced Ichabod Crane bombarded by thirty years of fluorescent light.

Well into the third week I was wading down a particularly fast, narrow section of the river and spotted a man sitting down in a pool below a long run. At first, my instinct was to move into the woods and go well around him, avoiding him as I had avoided all the others. But he was merely sitting, holding his hands in the water.

He was old, but not elderly. White-haired, close-cropped. His face had the markings of old ice, deeply lined and pocked by the sun. I was sure he hadn't noticed me when he said, matter-of-factly, "These fish have stories on them, you know." And then he lifted a fish almost out of the river, holding it in that thin layer between the water and the sky. I stepped into the water next to him, transfixed.

"And this fish," he said, "this fish tells me about the weather. Coming in for the winter. The way the spots come together sweeping up over the fin, that tells me snow. Much snow. The markings will tell you a lot if you let them," he said and then he released the fish in a motion I can only describe as how one might give a gift to a friend.

I watched him catch another fish, pointing with his finger, "See these spots," he said, "these bright greens, how close together they are, these fish have traveled through bear country." Once, he said, on the Columbia, he had seen a salmon whose skin told him the river below, all the way to the sea, was dying, and that he needed to drink some of the last good water before it was gone.

Then, motioning me closer, he whispered, "Perhaps one of these fish will reveal the way into the next life," then he ran his forearm under the water, arching it like a fish against the current.

That night, near my fire, he kept me awake telling me what I know now was the long story. I followed him through a coursing, plunging tale of his life . . . a boyhood of wandering with his family, Asian deserts, the foothills of the Himalayas, and then a long pilgrimage into the Northwest, living and hiking the salmon streams of the Oregon coast. What it came down to, when he had finished, was the fish. Reading the fish. His entire adult life spent traveling streams and rivers finding fish to read.

The next morning he had risen early and that was the last I saw of him. I looked up and down the river but found no tracks. All day I sat in the same spot he had been in. I cupped my hands and waited but nothing happened. Once, I felt the slight pressure of a fish flash through my hands, but came up with nothing.

When I lay in my tent that night I listened to the wind in the high canopy of the trees. I imagined his voice, or thought I heard it but it was only the wind. I thought of him then, sitting in the rush of the July river reading the skins of brook trout and fell asleep.

On the way home I stopped at a friend's cabin on the upper North Branch of the AuSable. I knew there were hundreds of brook trout moving in the river, each one carrying some story on its skin. For a moment that grew into an afternoon, I sat on his deck and imagined whittling myself into pieces, throwing each piece over the lawn into the river. I felt myself vanish that afternoon, my life crystallized around one particular vibrant spot, on one particular brook trout. My life only a particle in the story an old man might read on the side of a fish.

All the way home in the car I felt a pull in my jaw, how it seemed to grow and hook, my face contorting against the current washing through the memory of my life, my spine undulating like a fin. In three weeks I had accomplished what I had set out to do. Somewhere in the northern sections of Crawford County I had shed a life into the river. I slowed the car to watch huge cumulus clouds drift through the river of the sky. In the rearview mirror my eyes turned luminous. And for an instant I saw the way the world writes what it is trying to be: in clouds, in waves, in the wash of streams and on the skins of fish. I felt parts of myself come back into my body, the flecks of my eyes collecting like sediment, until I felt whole again, the river pulsing against the net of my skin.

THE WAGER

There was an older man and a younger one, then. Both of them given over to the ritual of opening day. They exchanged small gifts—a box of flies for the older one, a new line for the younger. Then, as they had done every opening day for the last twenty years, they walked to the window and stared out into the woods. There was an early morning mist. It was that last Saturday in April when both men sensed in each other that pull in the imagination, replaying each pool and run a hundredfold in the brief time they looked toward the river.

Now the low morning sun was shining in the windows, glinting off the dishes on the table. There were two places. The older one would sit at the end farthest from the kitchen while the younger one would sit at the opposite end of the table. They sat down and exchanged a few words at first, being careful, as men often are, not to break the religion of the moment. Were this a painting, both would appear pensive, tentative, as if the moment might somehow escape and there would be no fishing, no summers or seasons together on the river. They drank their wine slowly. A plum wine always reserved for this one morning in spring. There would be pancakes, and hard-cooked bacon, crisp and dry, the way they both liked it.

It was not a day for stories, and each man had grown accustomed to the silence of the other. They rose from the table and cleared the dishes into the sink. It was then that the younger one noticed the two small glasses on the back of the counter filled with clear water and a layer of tiny insects on the bottom. The older one explained that he had found them in the stomachs of two browns he had caught earlier in the morning. "Nymphs," he said, "probably Hendrickson's." And the younger one drew closer, lifted the glass in the light and looked at the perfection of their tiny legs, their minute wing cases bulging slightly.

Then, there came what they now refer to as "the wager," which linked them forever into a fraternity of two. The older one took the glass from the younger, raised it to his mouth, and took a long, slow drink, first the water, then entire bottom contents. "Nymphs," he said, "are good luck," placing the empty glass lightly on the counter.

Before the younger one could speak, the older one set the challenge. "We fish for two hours, streamers, on the short section from Pine Road to the flats. Once back, if your catch is smallest, you drink the second glass. If I lose, the Summers is yours."

For a long moment the word *Summers* stuck in his head. *Summers*, and already he began to build images of the finest rod he had ever seen resting in his hand, casting even more exquisitely than the older one had taught.

Outside, on the porch, they gathered up their gear, talked the small talk of fishermen about to enter holy experience, then stood for a moment face to face, to shake hands, offer good luck. At the end of the ritual, the younger one looked straight into the older one. "You're on," he mumbled, and headed out.

Once at the river, the older one took the lead as he always did. Each cast took him into the tightest pockets, the best runs. He laid out line in slow motion, and the younger one watched for several minutes before he let him get out of sight around the first bend.

For a long time the younger one strained and worked on his rod. He "put" the line places instead of letting it find its place, as the older one had shown. For an hour he fished in what he thought were good pockets, the streamer dancing in the dark water. Several times he felt the mouths of fish but came up with nothing.

Once around the bend he looked downriver for the older one. Nothing. No trace, as if the fog had taken him in. Then, on a cedar sweeper he found a small, scrawled note: "20 inches. See you at the house in an hour."

Instantly, the younger one grew more boylike. He swallowed hard, imagining walking into the house without a fish, his throat already working against itself, preparing for the contents of the second glass. For a moment he felt himself almost crying, then he began to fish again, almost with a vengeance. He was working the streamer into impossible places, all the while imagining the older one holding the twenty-inch fish in his hands.

For the next half hour he attacked the spots the older one had shown him. The streamer was beginning to move more rhythmically. Then, half in dream, his eyes heavy from rising before the alarm went off at five, he felt the strike. Automatically, he raised the rod tip, letting the fish work back against the reel. All sign of the second glass had vanished. He was winning.

He reeled slowly, then lifted the fat brown into his net, unhooked it, and laid it down.

In the short brown grass on the bank he flattened the fish out, then took out his tape. Carefully, he surveyed its length, counting to himself, "sixteen . . . seventeen . . . eighteen . . . eighteen and a half . . . eighteen and three-quarters . . . damn . . . damn!" and he caught himself. It was over. He knew it. If he didn't lose because of his fish, he would lose on the clock. Quickly he laid the fish in his creel, stood up, and bolted off through the woods.

When he walked in the door, the older one was standing at the sink, his back toward him. "Well, I guess you lost," he said, and turned, grinning at the younger one.

"Here's one, at least, eighteen and three-quarters, but it's not over twenty. Gimme the glass."

The older one stopped his hand. "Just a minute," he said, "take a look."

For a second the younger one stared into the sink. He counted to himself: one . . . two. And there in the basin lay two perfectly speckled ten-inch brook trout.

"Twenty inches," the older one said under his breath.

"But . . . but," the younger stammered, reaching for the glass, his face contorted into disgust and loss.

"No, it's not really fair. A trick isn't a win. Here, take the rod."

The younger one held out his hand and felt the bamboo come to life. For five minutes he said nothing, moving his hands up and down the length of the cane, turning it, then reading the older one's name inscribed on the butt plate.

"Now it's yours," the older said. "You earned it."

He held the rod for a long time, half smiling, almost weeping. Then, in a rush of movement, almost as if swirling toward something both seen and unseen, almost as if striking the glass, the younger raised it to his lips, drank in the water first, then the nymphs, slapping it down in front of the older one as he finished.

WHAT MY FATHER TOLD ME

What my father told me, he mostly told me when we were fishing. It didn't matter that we had skipped church for the hundredth time, or whether he had walked into my school and gotten me out of class. He wanted to tell me things, he said, and the best place, he felt, was on the river. He said the river was as close to time as you were going to get. No sense, he said, watching a clock to learn about time. It wouldn't even do you any good to study rock stratification or fossils, as some scientists believed.

What seemed to arrest my father's attention most was the fact that rivers were always full of water. He would often stand on the banks of our cabin on the North Branch and ask over and over where all that water was coming from. Of course, he knew. And one summer when it was over 90 for almost two weeks in a row, we sweated our way north of Lovells and found the source: a small fingerlet seeping out from under a hummock in a swamp. Another time we stopped along the mainstream and my father showed me what he called a sacred spot. There was an iron ring in the ground, and looking into it was like peering into the eye of a river god, my father whispered.

My father taught me about perfection, too. Often I heard him say "perfect, everything is perfect" and when I asked what he meant, he'd always say, "Just look around." But I remember him telling me a story about perfection, just to illustrate that perfection wasn't always an absolute quality in his life. Once in Montana he been fishing a section of the Madison when he stopped in mid-cast to admire what he considered to be absolute perfection: a clear, evening sky, five-pound rainbows rising to midges, alone and miles from any house. Suddenly he heard the sound of tires squealing, the crush of metal against the guardrail a hundred feet above him and a Ford Pinto flew over the exact spot where he was fishing, landed in the river and sank in front of him. The driver swam toward him, my father half cursing his bad luck, but marveling at his one chance to see a car fly.

He taught me about glaciers and about how glaciers literally carved out the bellies of rivers. Move this water out of here he'd say, and all you got is a meandering single track through the woods barely deep enough to spit in, but add water and you've got a living vein. My father never talked much about God or religion except to say that whatever made rivers had to be wild.

My father loved wildness. He loved the fact that you could stand only so long in the current of a river until your feet started to drop out from under you. And he often said, over his shoulder when we were fishing together, that you could take something out of your imagination you didn't like, just as you would out of your pocket and let it go into the river and it would never come back.

He told me that whenever he felt any sense of failure, he would go to the river and just let whatever was bothering him loose in the water. He said he felt wild when he drank from the river, or caught brook trout and ate them on the same day. Trout particles, he called them and he was sure they had lodged in his bloodstream over the years until, he said proudly, he was more brook trout than man.

When I was twelve he took me to the Upper Peninsula for a fishing trip on the Big Two-Hearted. He was careful to point out that the river wasn't the real river Hemingway was writing about, that was the Black, further east of the Two-Hearted. This was before the Mackinaw Bridge, when you had to take a ferry across the Straits. We holed up in the station wagon, listening to Ernie Harwell call a late Tigers game. I could smell the odor of wet canvas. Tents and fishing bags. Fishing tackle.

On our way into the river my father told me that of all the places he'd been, all the rivers he'd fished, this place we were going meant the most. In the 40's, he and Fred Lewis had fished this water for weeks at a time. Years later, when Fred went blind, his wife dropped him off and he fished by himself for two weeks.

I still have pictures of Fred Lewis in my albums at home. In one, he's wearing a red plaid wool shirt. My dad says those were the best shirts you could wear to fish in. He told me to always have a fishing shirt handy. Never wear it for anything else, he said. And never, never wash it. If you can, he said, the first time you wear it, you need to anoint it with the blood of a few night crawlers and brook trout.

That's what my father fished for most. Brook trout. He could sneak into the smallest, brushiest streams where you'd swear there wouldn't hardly be any water. He'd dangle a short rod over the bank and slip the worm in without making a ripple. Then he'd mutter a prayer to the fish gods, to keep them close, he'd say, and then he'd lift the tip of his rod so slowly you couldn't see. I remember brook trout coming out of the clear water, how they looked like miniature paintings vibrant and loose with color.

My father told me, sitting on the banks of the Two-Hearted, that the best way to cook brook trout was in the coals. Pack them in river clay, he said and put it in the fire. When the clay cracked, the fish was done.

We ate fish like that for a week. My father drinking small glasses of wine. Sometimes he'd let me sip some and we'd lean back against the trees, our faces hot from the flames. Coming through the fire, his voice sounded like the voice of a god. It sounded hollow and large, as if it were coming from somewhere under the earth.

My father told me that rivers weren't really natural phenomena at all. Rivers, he said came directly out of the veins of the gods themselves. To prove it, he said, try to follow one. When you tromp through a swamp for a day or two, following something that's getting smaller and smaller and then finally vanishes under a hummock in some swamp somewhere, he said, you'd need to go down under the earth to find the source.

The source was in wildness, he said. A wild god making a river come up out of the ground by opening up one of his veins and letting his divine blood sift upward toward blue sky. When I think about my father now, I think about gods under the earth and about blood, about how he baptized himself there on the Two-Hearted that summer.

I'd already been baptized twice. Once in church when I was a baby, he said. But he'd had second thoughts about what went on, about who was sanctifying what. And another time by my grandfather with a handful of lake water. Now, he told me, I needed to drink from the same river that he drank from.

We were standing knee deep just about the mouth. Lake Superior was crashing below us. He lifted a cupped hand to my mouth and I drank and then he drank. Blood, he whispered. Keep this wild blood in you for the rest of your life.

When my father wasn't working or fishing, his other great joy was quoting short lines of poetry while we fished. When he wasn't talking about the connection between rivers and the spiritual territory he tended so seriously inside me, he was talking about the wildness he loved in poets he'd read. I always thought it odd that a man brought up around huge tool and die presses would come to something as seemingly fragile as poetry. He particularly loved an ancient Irish poem, "The Wild Man Comes to the

Monastery." Some nights when he was a bend or two below me I could hear him calling back, "though you like the fat and meat which are eaten in the drinking halls, I like better to eat a head of clean watercress in a place without sorrow." At twelve, those lines meant little, but over the years, something seeped in and built up, an accumulation of images, he liked to say to me, would get me through the hard times when my life would go dark. To keep away the loneliness he'd say and then whisper another line from Machado, or Neruda. Keep these poets close to your heart, he would admonish me and so I fished for years listening to the great Spanish surrealists drifting upriver to me in the dark.

Weeks later we were drifting on Turk Lake trolling for pike. It was almost dark and my father was looking back over the transom, watching his line. One word came out of his mouth. Storm. I looked into the western sky and saw huge clouds boiling in, black and inky, the curl of them like a huge wave. Keep fishing he said. Keep casting from the bow. The pike will feed just before it hits, keep casting, cast your heart out, he said.

From where I stood I could see a white belly slashing up toward my lure. I could see my father etched by lightning, his rod low, then him striking, both of us fighting fish under the darkening sky.

We lost both fish. The sky seemed to literally fall on us. My father told me later in the cabin, that we'd been lucky, foolish, but lucky he said. He told me that luck was when skill met necessity and that his lightning theory was worth proving. Besides, he said, we had fished in the wildness of a storm, and what better way to end a day than to be wringing the wildness out of your wet clothes, sucking the wild rain out of your cuff, thirsty for more.

What went into a boy, stayed inside. I hid it away, kept my father's voice inside me, packed in close to my heart. Whatever my father told me I always regarded as the absolute truth. I believed in the river gods. Believed that river water came from their veins; that if there was one god, He must be made entirely of water. That was years ago. For years I kept lists and journals of what I remembered my father telling me. It was all good.

Take the river inside as you would a text he would tell me more than once. He knew that once inside you could memorize every pool and run, every rock in a stream and unless there was a winter of bad anchor ice, you could come back in the spring for opening day and look for every mark you'd imagined in the winter. Even better, he told me, was the ability to enter the river inside whenever you felt the need to. "I got to light out for the territory" he was fond of saying, a good part of him given over to the wildest parts of Huck Finn's personality. And always there was that dark, brooding sense of the surreal, the river looming up inside both of us as if it were alive and breathing through our skins.

But, what I remember most clearly now is the way his voice sounded on the day he died. He was barely coherent, wandering through the double stupor of morphine and the cancer in his head. He was almost dead, but you could tell his mind was still reeling with images. On this last day he was talking rivers, and trips he'd taken. I showed him a new reel and he launched himself into a beautiful story about fishing the Two-Hearted again. Then, he said he had been overtaken the night before by a dream that he had turned into something purely wild. He didn't know what it was, he said, but he knew he had moved with grace, and that he moved under the earth with great force. He said that when he woke up, he felt a part of him was missing and that he had some sense in the dream that he had been deposited somewhere. Surely, he said, he must have dreamed himself into a river. He knew, and I remember him telling me, that there were Sioux Indians who could turn themselves into rivers. He said he had seen one such man when he was a boy traveling through Nebraska with his father. The Sioux had simply lain down, begun singing in low tones, stretching himself out further and further until he literally flowed past his feet.

My father's last dream had taken him back to that day, back to that wondrous opportunity to see flesh transcend itself. Now my father, weak from disease, lay still in his bed, only his mouth moving. What he told me on that last day was to honor my promise to take him away, to take him back to the river.

I remember my father telling me he had scouted years for the spot. He was never one for fanfare, or ceremony, and the measure of a good day was calculated by hard work. A good spot had requirements he had said: shade most of the day, a gravel bottom and a mixture of currents, a mixing place. We visited only once. That afternoon he sat with me and talked mostly of dams. It was either a wing dam, he thought, or more probably a coffer dam.

In the sunlight that filtered through the trees he drew diagrams in the dirt. Head the river off gently, he said, or it would surge over everything. With leaves he made the wash of the river, traced it exactly over the spot where he wanted the grave. Mud he said, the trunks of trees jammed by the current against steel rods driven into the bed of the river to hold back the water. He was firm about this desire, and his firmness carried itself into the waking dreams I had of the dam, the daily visions I had of myself felling trees, driving the steel rods, packing mud like a beaver.

After he died I simply carried him off from the funeral parlor, out the back door and into the truck. His friends buried the coffin in the cemetery on the hill and I drove his body to the river.

I worked most of the first day cutting. The trees came down on the bank and I moved over their limbs as if the saw were a scythe. He lay up higher on the bank, his head on a rock as if he were sleeping. I drove the stakes in two feet of water, then rolled the trees in, guiding their huge trunks against the stakes.

That night I worked against the river, my hands digging up river stones, mud, clay from the banks. I looked often at him lying up above me, his face barely visible in the cast of light from the lantern. I had made the cuts like he had instructed. Like putting a log cabin together, he had motioned in the dirt that day, one log grooved, the other mortised. The seam of the logs joining together was barely a scar against my hands.

I slept off and on, working, sleeping. Packing mud and clay, repacking small spots where the water wanted to get in. When I finished, I was standing in something that looked like a wooden arm growing out of the bank and angling back against the flow of the river. At the lip of the dam I held my hand against the water, then turned back to look at the moist bottom of the river below me, open to daylight.

I dug down below grade, through rocks and smaller rocks, into the clay that cradled the river, the water seeping into the grave.

No mumbo-jumbo he had said, no remorse, just let me go back. I laid him face up at first, then rolled him to his side so one ear might be toward the river, the other toward the sky. I packed him in, tight he had said, wedged into the bottom of the river and then I covered him, first with clay and heavy stones, then with lighter rocks and pebbles.

I waited until early evening, lit the lantern and then began dismantling the dam, only enough to let the water in, letting two logs drift away in the darkening current. The water sluiced over the dam, now inches under water, over the stones, and sifted down, I am sure into my father's lips. I wanted to speak something to him in the dark, but couldn't. He had wanted silence; wanted the sound of the river all around us.

Now, in summer, I drift over his spot. The remnants of the dam still hold. I imagine my father has gone back completely by now, and only his bones are held in the belly of the river. I think of him often, how he carried me far beyond the years he could. How his life merged and moved with mine and then swept in another direction. I think of him alive and casting, examining and selecting flies like a surgeon, his love of poems and wildness fused together and fueled by his desire to take in all of the world in front of him. I think of how his life comes back to me each time I fish, each time I step into the current. Mostly, I think of how both of us are carried by rivers, how his memory sifts through me like the current where only his bones are left to tell the story.

LAST POOL

I suppose, now that I'm telling this, no one will believe me. I'll admit to the far-fetched notion of it: finding a place where trout, big trout, would spend their last days. After all, how many of us have seen a trout die a natural death? Can you even think of the time when you looked down and saw a fish holding, his body perfect, only to roll suddenly away with the current, surfacing downstream, his white belly pointed toward the sky? On the skin of it, this story sounds as if it's about elephants. Graveyards.

But I was there. Stood at the pool myself and watched the sun arc through a whole day while below me I watched the spotted backs of eight-pound browns shift in the slow sifting of current. I was, and am still, stupefied. Standing there, I measured my own senses. I thought I knew exactly where I had traversed the three bends of the river before it turned near the edge of the swamp. I was further sure, I kept telling myself, that I was truly still on Simpson Creek. The Simpson Creek that passes through miles of cedar deadfall and hummocks, trickling past mucky banks only to move its three-foot width into the AuSable without even a ripple.

In my head I sensed my position as if I were standing in front of a topographical map and I had driven a pin into this place and said, "here, I am exactly here." But I was wrong. I was on a creek, I think now, that has no name. I had wandered in well before daylight and gotten turned around somehow and found myself standing still in the swamp, just listening.

At first light I moved north to where I thought Simpson Creek might be, but found myself, standing, miraculously, on the edge of a pool perhaps ten feet across and no more than eight feet deep. The roots of huge cedars swept into it like fingers. More than a wide spot in a small stream, it looked like a spring of sorts. The bottom sand bubbled in places and fish moved in and out from under the bank. I counted thirty or forty fish, not sure they were all different, but sure they were large, larger, I knew, than any fish I had ever seen in the river.

I began to ask questions of myself: how . . . no, why had I found this place? For several minutes, which might have been an hour, I decided it was pure Providence, then I danced over to the side of luck and then back again.

I stayed with luck and good fortune as I put my rod together, then fingered over a ragged book of nymphs. I couldn't very well float a dry fly to deep-cruising browns. In a clear pool. With no current on top. So I tied the most careful of knots on the smallest of tippets I could manage, then stepped back from the pool to regain what little composure I had left.

I was trembling at this one single chance I had stumbled upon, or been given and I hesitated. Not wanting to spook the fish out of the pool, I knelt first and then crawled back, just as I had done as a child brook trout fishing with my father on the brushy streams near Greenville . Back then, we whispered and dropped our tiny hooks with leaf worms threaded onto them and we prayed. I actually heard my father praying over the bank of a small trout stream in Michigan. He prayed to his mother and to his father, and then he prayed to the god of fish.

So I lay there on the side of the pool, trying to recall the fish prayer of my father. I thought about the water and the angle I wanted the nymph to follow as it drifted toward bottom. When I inched close enough to look, most of the fish had steadied, almost motionless, an inch or two off the sandy bottom.

I watched for a while, wanting to know precisely where to set the nymph so it would look like a nymph falling, almost like a feather, through the clear water. In my mind I hooked, of course, the largest fish I could see and just as I began to reel him in I saw a fish suddenly roll up, as if it were taking a fly on the surface, only it went suddenly still. Then it turned belly-up and floated to the surface of the pool, its gills moving almost imperceptibly.

I watched it circle the pool in the slow eddy of current and then it died completely. When it caught the full light of midday, its colors had already started to fade. The other fish paid no attention. They moved up and down in the spring, banked slowly for tiny nymphs and then settled back down.

I stayed for an hour, maybe two. I watched the sun track through the trees. I moved back from the pool and drank an entire flask of whiskey. I looked repeatedly at my tackle. I ran my finger down the humped back of the nymph I'd wanted to use, imagined it so perfectly wet and deadly. Then I left.

I hadn't fished. It took hours to thrash my way out. I stood at the car and offered the prayer I had forgotten in my adrenaline haste. I looked at the sky. I looked at my hands. I put my rod away and drove home. In front of me the road turned slick in an early evening rain. In the rearview mirror the sky darkened and seemed ever closer. I tried to remember the way in, knowing the way memory has of closing up, turning the past into myth, tangling details into snarls of fact and fiction, then praised myself for not marking the way out.

TITLES IN THE GREAT LAKES BOOKS SERIES

Freshwater Fury: Yarns and Reminiscences of the Greatest Storm in Inland Navigation, by Frank Barcus, 1986 (reprint)

Call It North Country: The Story of Upper Michigan, by John Bartlow Martin, 1986 (reprint)

The Land of the Crooked Tree, by U. P. Hedrick, 1986 (reprint)

Michigan Place Names, by Walter Romig, 1986 (reprint)

Luke Karamazov, by Conrad Hilberry, 1987

The Late, Great Lakes: An Environmental History, by William Ashworth, 1987 (reprint)

Great Pages of Michigan History from the Detroit Free Press, 1987

Waiting for the Morning Train: An American Boyhood, by Bruce Catton, 1987 (reprint)

Michigan Voices: Our State's History in the Words of the People Who Lived It, compiled and edited by Joe Grimm, 1987

Danny and the Boys, Being Some Legends of Hungry Hollow, by Robert Traver, 1987 (reprint)

Hanging On, or How to Get through a Depression and Enjoy Life, by Edmund G. Love, 1987 (reprint)

The Situation in Flushing, by Edmund G. Love, 1987 (reprint)

A Small Bequest, by Edmund G. Love, 1987 (reprint)

The Saginaw Paul Bunyan, by James Stevens, 1987 (reprint)

The Ambassador Bridge: A Monument to Progress, by Philip P. Mason, 1988

Let the Drum Beat: A History of the Detroit Light Guard, by Stanley D. Solvick, 1988

An Afternoon in Waterloo Park, by Gerald Dumas, 1988 (reprint)

Contemporary Michigan Poetry: Poems from the Third Coast, edited by Michael Delp, Conrad Hilberry and Herbert Scott, 1988

Over the Graves of Horses, by Michael Delp, 1988

Wolf in Sheep's Clothing: The Search for a Child Killer, by Tommy McIntyre, 1988

Copper-Toed Boots, by Marguerite de Angeli, 1989 (reprint)

Detroit Images: Photographs of the Renaissance City, edited by John J. Bukow-
czyk and Douglas Aikenhead, with Peter Slavcheff, 1989

Hangdog Reef: Poems Sailing the Great Lakes, by Stephen Tudor, 1989

Detroit: City of Race and Class Violence, revised edition, by B. J. Widick, 1989

Deep Woods Frontier: A History of Logging in Northern Michigan, by Theodore J.
Karamanski, 1989

Orvie, The Dictator of Dearborn, by David L. Good, 1989

Seasons of Grace: A History of the Catholic Archdiocese of Detroit, by Leslie
Woodcock Tentler, 1990

The Pottery of John Foster: Form and Meaning, by Gordon and Elizabeth Orear,
1990

The Diary of Bishop Frederic Baraga: First Bishop of Marquette, Michigan,
edited by Regis M. Walling and Rev. N. Daniel Rupp, 1990

Walnut Pickles and Watermelon Cake: A Century of Michigan Cooking, by Larry
B. Massie and Priscilla Massie, 1990

The Making of Michigan, 1820–1860: A Pioneer Anthology, edited by Justin L.
Kestenbaum, 1990

America's Favorite Homes: A Guide to Popular Early Twentieth-Century Homes,
by Robert Schweitzer and Michael W. R. Davis, 1990

Beyond the Model T: The Other Ventures of Henry Ford, by Ford R. Bryan, 1990

Life after the Line, by Josie Kearns, 1990

*Michigan Lumbertowns: Lumbermen and Laborers in Saginaw, Bay City, and
Muskegon, 1870–1905,* by Jeremy W. Kilar, 1990

Detroit Kids Catalog: The Hometown Tourist, by Ellyce Field, 1990

Waiting for the News, by Leo Litwak, 1990 (reprint)

Detroit Perspectives, edited by Wilma Wood Henrickson, 1991

Life on the Great Lakes: A Wheelsman's Story, by Fred W. Dutton, edited by
William Donohue Ellis, 1991

Copper Country Journal: The Diary of Schoolmaster Henry Hobart, 1863–1864,
by Henry Hobart, edited by Philip P. Mason, 1991

John Jacob Astor: Business and Finance in the Early Republic, by John Denis
Haeger, 1991

Survival and Regeneration: Detroit's American Indian Community, by Edmund J.
Danziger, Jr., 1991

Steamboats and Sailors of the Great Lakes, by Mark L. Thompson, 1991

Cobb Would Have Caught It: The Golden Age of Baseball in Detroit, by Richard
Bak, 1991

Michigan in Literature, by Clarence Andrews, 1992

Under the Influence of Water: Poems, Essays, and Stories, by Michael Delp, 1992

The Country Kitchen, by Della T. Lutes, 1992 (reprint)

The Making of a Mining District: Keweenaw Native Copper 1500–1870, by David J. Krause, 1992

Kids Catalog of Michigan Adventures, by Ellyce Field, 1993

Henry's Lieutenants, by Ford R. Bryan, 1993

Historic Highway Bridges of Michigan, by Charles K. Hyde, 1993

Lake Erie and Lake St. Clair Handbook, by Stanley J. Bolsenga and Charles E. Herndendorf, 1993

Queen of the Lakes, by Mark Thompson, 1994

Iron Fleet: The Great Lakes in World War II, by George J. Joachim, 1994

Turkey Stearnes and the Detroit Stars: The Negro Leagues in Detroit, 1919–1933, by Richard Bak, 1994

Pontiac and the Indian Uprising, by Howard H. Peckham, 1994 (reprint)

Charting the Inland Seas: A History of the U.S. Lake Survey, by Arthur M. Woodford, 1994 (reprint)

Ojibwa Narratives of Charles and Charlotte Kawbawgam and Jacques LePique, 1893–1895. Recorded with Notes by Homer H. Kidder, edited by Arthur P. Bourgeois, 1994, co-published with the Marquette County Historical Society

Strangers and Sojourners: A History of Michigan's Keweenaw Peninsula, by Arthur W. Thurner, 1994

Win Some, Lose Some: G. Mennen Williams and the New Democrats, by Helen Washburn Berthelot, 1995

Sarkis, by Gordon and Elizabeth Orear, 1995

The Northern Lights: Lighthouses of the Upper Great Lakes, by Charles K. Hyde, 1995 (reprint)

Kids Catalog of Michigan Adventures, second edition, by Ellyce Field, 1995

Rumrunning and the Roaring Twenties: Prohibition on the Michigan-Ontario Waterway, by Philip P. Mason, 1995

In the Wilderness with the Red Indians, by E. R. Baierlein, translated by Anita Z. Boldt, edited by Harold W. Moll, 1996

Elmwood Endures: History of a Detroit Cemetery, by Michael Franck, 1996

Master of Precision: Henry M. Leland, by Mrs. Wilfred C. Leland with Minnie Dubbs Millbrook, 1996 (reprint)

Haul-Out: New and Selected Poems, by Stephen Tudor, 1996

Kids Catalog of Michigan Adventures, third edition, by Ellyce Field, 1997

Beyond the Model T: The Other Ventures of Henry Ford, revised edition, by Ford R. Bryan, 1997

Young Henry Ford: A Picture History of the First Forty Years, by Sidney Olson, 1997 (reprint)

The Coast of Nowhere: Meditations on Rivers, Lakes and Streams, by Michael Delp, 1997

From Saginaw Valley to Tin Pan Alley: Saginaw's Contribution to American Popular Music, 1890–1955, by R. Grant Smith, 1998

The Long Winter Ends, by Newton G. Thomas, 1998 (reprint)

Bridging the River of Hatred: The Pioneering Efforts of Detroit Police Commissioner George Edwards, by Mary M. Stolberg, 1998

Toast of the Town: The Life and Times of Sunnie Wilson, by Sunnie Wilson with John Cohassey, 1998

These Men Have Seen Hard Service: The First Michigan Sharpshooters in the Civil War, by Raymond J. Herek, 1998

A Place for Summer: One Hundred Years at Michigan and Trumbull, by Richard Bak, 1998

Early Midwestern Travel Narratives: An Annotated Bibliography, 1634–1850, by Robert R. Hubach, 1998 (reprint)

All-American Anarchist: Joseph A. Labadie and the Labor Movement, by Carlotta R. Anderson, 1998

Michigan in the Novel, 1816–1996: An Annotated Bibliography, by Robert Beasecker, 1998

"Time by Moments Steals Away": The 1848 Journal of Ruth Douglass, by Robert L. Root, Jr., 1998

The Detroit Tigers: A Pictorial Celebration of the Greatest Players and Moments in Tigers' History, updated edition, by William M. Anderson, 1999

Father Abraham's Children: Michigan Episodes in the Civil War, by Frank B. Woodford, 1999 (reprint)

Letter from Washington, 1863–1865, by Lois Bryan Adams, edited and with an introduction by Evelyn Leasher, 1999

Wonderful Power: The Story of Ancient Copper Working in the Lake Superior Basin, by Susan R. Martin, 1999

A Sailor's Logbook: A Season aboard Great Lakes Freighters, by Mark L. Thompson, 1999

Huron: The Seasons of a Great Lake, by Napier Shelton, 1999

Tin Stackers: The History of the Pittsburgh Steamship Company, by Al Miller, 1999

Art in Detroit Public Places, revised edition, text by Dennis Nawrocki, photographs by David Clements, 1999

Brewed in Detroit: Breweries and Beers Since 1830, by Peter H. Blum, 1999

Detroit Kids Catalog: A Family Guide for the 21st Century, by Ellyce Field, 2000

"Expanding the Frontiers of Civil Rights": Michigan, 1948–1968, by Sidney Fine, 2000

Graveyard of the Lakes, by Mark L. Thompson, 2000

Enterprising Images: The Goodridge Brothers, African American Photographers, 1847–1922, by John Vincent Jezierski, 2000

New Poems from the Third Coast: Contemporary Michigan Poetry, edited by Michael Delp, Conrad Hilberry, and Josie Kearns, 2000

Arab Detroit: From Margin to Mainstream, edited by Nabeel Abraham and Andrew Shryock, 2000

The Sandstone Architecture of the Lake Superior Region, by Kathryn Bishop Eckert, 2000

Looking Beyond Race: The Life of Otis Milton Smith, by Otis Milton Smith and Mary M. Stolberg, 2000

Mail by the Pail, by Colin Bergel, illustrated by Mark Koenig, 2000

Great Lakes Journey: A New Look at America's Freshwater Coast, by William Ashworth, 2000

A Life in the Balance: The Memoirs of Stanley J. Winkelman, by Stanley J. Winkelman, 2000

Schooner Passage: Sailing Ships and the Lake Michigan Frontier, by Theodore J. Karamanski, 2000

The Outdoor Museum: The Magic of Michigan's Marshall M. Fredericks, by Marcy Heller Fisher, illustrated by Christine Collins Woomer, 2001

Detroit in Its World Setting: A Three Hundred Year Chronology, 1701–2001, edited by David Lee Poremba, 2001

Frontier Metropolis: Picturing Early Detroit, 1701–1838, by Brian Leigh Dunnigan, 2001

Michigan Remembered: Photographs from the Farm Security Administration and the Office of War Information, 1936–1943, edited by Constance B. Schulz, with Introductory Essays by Constance B. Schulz and William H. Mulligan, Jr., 2001

This Is Detroit, 1701–2001, by Arthur M. Woodford, 2001

History of the Finns in Michigan, by Armas K. E. Holmio, translated by Ellen M. Ryynanen, 2001

Angels in the Architecture: A Photographic Elegy to an American Asylum, by Heidi Johnson, 2001

For an updated listing of books in this series, please visit our Web site at http://wsupress.wayne.edu